TROUBLEMAKERS

Troublemakers

VOLUME 1

Rebekah Brewster

Quietbeauty Publishing

Contents

1 William and Ellen Craft   1

2 Lewis Hayden   21

3 James Oglethorpe   54

4 John Wesley   68

5 Owen Lovejoy   90

6 John P. Hale   114

7 John Brown   126

Bibliography   180

References   194

Bible Versions   202

About The Author   203

Dedication

This book is dedicated to YOU
as you stand strong for the truth during troubled times.

Never give up while you are suffering
because you are tougher and stronger
than anything the world can do to you.

"No weapon formed against you shall prosper,
and you will refute every tongue that accuses you.
This is the heritage of the servants of the LORD,
and their vindication is from Me,' declares the LORD."
Isaiah 54:17 (BSB)

Note to Readers

For much of American history,
the people who wanted to destroy (abolish) slavery were called
abolitionists.

This book continues the stories and characters studied in
Christians That Fought Slavery
so we encourage you to read that book first
for the full historical background.

Legal Disclaimer

This book is the author's personal opinion and Christian faith.

The author does not speak for any organization or other person.

This book is history and entertainment.

This book is NOT legal, tax, medical or investment advice.

Please do not use anything in this book to make a bad decision, break the law, or commit violence.

Any description in this book of violence, breaking laws or bad behavior is so we can learn from history.

Please understand that even historians disagree on what happened in history so while this book was researched and believed to be true, there are no guarantees.

Some quotes have been edited for clarity, brevity and to reflect modern English.

Please understand that in this book each character speaks for themselves and their personal opinion does not necessarily reflect the author's opinion. Sometimes there is some very strong language in this book when the characters feel it is necessary to use it.

Reader discretion is advised.

Image Credits

All images in this book are courtesy of the Library of Congress and believed to be in the public domain unless otherwise specified.

The front cover image is a painting by Henry Alexander Ogden (1856-1936) titled "Independent Company Organizations."

The painting shows how American soldiers dressed in different ways during the Revolutionary War and is also probably how James Oglethorpe's soldiers would have dressed.

The back cover image is a painting by Henry Alexander Ogden titled "Infantry Continential Army 1779-1783."

These two images show the background of what warriors looked like during the time period of this book.

1

William and Ellen Craft

"Be strong in the Lord and in His mighty power.
Put on the full armor of God
so that you can make your stand against the devil's schemes."
Ephesians 6:10-11 (BSB)

William Craft
1824-1900

Ellen Craft
1826-1891

From Georgia

When William and Ellen Craft heard the *Declaration of Independence*, it changed their lives. They realized that they had rights. Growing up in the United States of America, they had known nothing but slavery.

William later wrote, *"As slaves we heard Acts 17:26, 'God has made all nations of one blood.'"*

"We heard 'All men are created equal and endowed by their Creator with rights to life, liberty, and the pursuit of happiness.'"

"So we felt justified in running a thousand miles to obtain those rights."[1]

Years later when William wrote his autobiography, he described their early years. *"My wife and I were born in different towns in Georgia."[2]*

At a young age they were both sold away from their own families and sent to live in the city of Macon, Georgia.

They grew up working for different masters. William became a highly skilled carpenter, who worked for a cabinet maker, but was not allowed to keep most of his own wages. Yet working that job gave him some freedom to come and go without having to ask permission.

Meanwhile, Ellen worked as a maid for the family of a doctor. She was given her own room but not allowed to leave the house without permission.

One day she was sent on an errand into town. She saw the handsome William Craft. They fell in love at first sight. They got married but could not live together because they belonged to different masters. All they could do is cherish whatever brief visits they had together.

William visited Ellen as often as he could. The rest of the time he missed her and counted the moments until they could be together again.

Together they dreamed of freedom. Yet reality kept getting in their way. While they both wanted a family, they worried about how they could be separated at any moment. Both of them had already experienced the pain of being taken away from family.

There had to be a way out.

Yet how could they travel over 1,000 miles from Georgia to freedom in the north without getting caught? Buying a train ticket was impossible. Walking would take forever. Traveling by boat was forbidden. Renting a horse would raise too many questions.

As William later described, *"We thought of plan after plan but they all seemed too difficult. We knew it was unlawful for any public transportation to take us as passengers without our master's consent."*

"If we left without his consent, the professional slavehunters would have soon had their ferocious bloodhounds on our track."

"Nothing gives slaveholders more pleasure than capturing and torturing fugitives."

"We would be dragged back, separated, and punished with the worst labor or tortured to death to make an example to others."

"After puzzling our brains for years, we were reluctantly driven to the sad conclusion that it was almost impossible to travel over 1,000 miles to escape from slavery in Georgia."[3]

Then one day the answer came.

Masters were allowed to take slaves with them when they traveled across the country.

Ellen was very light skinned. As William described, *"My wife's first master was her father and her mother his slave. My wife is so white that she was often mistaken for being a child of the family."[4]* This had annoyed the lady of the house and she had sent Ellen away at eleven years old to work for another family. Years passed before Ellen met William and figured out how to escape.

William realized that Ellen could travel north on the train as a white passenger with her servant William to carry her luggage. Then they could buy train tickets with the money they had saved up.

Or so they hoped. Ellen wasn't sure the plan would work. Women normally did not travel by themselves. Everyone on the train would be suspicious to see a single woman traveling with a male servant, instead of with family members. What if someone they knew happened to be on the train and recognized them?

Plus, how could they even buy a train ticket? The trains were closely watched for escaping fugitives. Buying a ticket required proving that you could read and write by writing down your name and information.

Neither William or Ellen could read or write, since there were strict laws against educating slaves.

These laws were so strictly enforced that years later when William wrote his autobiography, he gave this example.

In 1854, Margaret Douglas was thrown in jail and fined in Virginia. Her crime was *"being an evil disposed person, moved by the devil, did wickedly teach a slave girl named Kate to read the Bible."*

The judge in the case told her, *"You are guilty of one of the vilest crimes that ever disgraced society. You have taught a slave girl to read the Bible. No enlightened society can exist with these crimes unpunished."*

"In other countries you would have paid for this crime by forfeiting your life. The court feels no sympathy for you and inflicts the utmost penalty of one month in the county jail and you must pay the costs of this prosecution." [5]

This was the evil system holding William and Ellen in bondage.

Even if they were able to buy a train ticket, the trip would take several days and include several overnight stops. How could they check into a hotel room? Wouldn't it look suspicious if they didn't follow the crowd when the train stopped along the way and all the other train passengers would be getting off the train and checking into hotels? Once again it seemed like there was no hope.

As Christmastime came in 1848, William and Ellen prayed to God for an answer. During the holidays, they would be granted a few days off from work. This was the only time of the year that they could have time to get away before they would be missed.

During that time, they figured out the plan. William later described, *"While sitting in our little room upon the verge of despair, all at once my wife raised her head, smiled and said, 'I think I have it!'"* [6]

What if she dressed up as a gentleman?

Ellen could disguise her smooth skin by wearing a hat, glasses, and covering her chin with a bandage. Then she could put her right hand in a sling and tell everyone that it was broken so she needed someone else to sign the registry for her.

Wearing a disguise would keep people from recognizing her. Then she could sit in the first-class train car where no one would be looking for fugitives. William could travel along in the economy car where slaves normally rode.

It was a brilliant idea. William immediately went out and tried to buy the disguise. That was the next problem. It was illegal for anyone to sell anything to a slave without their master's knowledge. However, there were plenty of people who needed money. So being very careful, William was able to find people who needed the money enough to break the law. *"I went to different parts of the town at odd times and purchased things piece by piece, except for the trousers which Ellen had to make. Then I took them to the house where my wife resided."*

William took the pieces to Ellen's room where she hid them in her dresser. William had built that dresser for her with hidden drawers that could be locked so no one would find it.

They worked really fast. Eight days after thinking of the plan, they were ready to do it. Late one night, Ellen turned to William and said, *"It's almost too much for us to do but I feel that God is on our side. With His help we will succeed."*[7]

William held her and promised that he would fight to his last breath to protect her. As he later described, *"When the time came for us to leave, we blew out the lights (candles), knelt down and prayed to our Heavenly Father to help us as He did His people of old to escape."*[8]

Very early in the morning, *"I took my wife by the hand, stepped softly to the door, raised the latch, drew it open and looked out. Everything appeared as silent as death. I locked the door and we tiptoed into the street, afraid to move or breath freely for fear the sleeping tyrants should awake and come down on us with double vengeance for daring to escape."*[9]

RISKING EVERYTHING TO ESCAPE

First, to be safe they split up and left in different directions for the train station. Once there, William directly boarded the economy car. Meanwhile, Ellen went to the ticket office to purchase the tickets.

Buying a train ticket to a northern city would seem suspicious. So instead, Ellen only bought tickets to travel two hundred miles to Savannah, Georgia. The plan was to keep buying new tickets along the train route without anyone realizing where they were actually headed. Then Ellen boarded the train and took her seat in the first-class car.

Time passed very slowly as they waited for the train to leave. William could only hope and pray that no one recognized them.

Just as the train was about to leave, William looked out the window. What he saw, made his heart stop beating.

Someone had already noticed that they were missing. The cabinet maker, who employed William, was running frantically toward the train. He stopped long enough to talk to the conductor, then he boarded the first-class car and began desperately searching. William knew there was only one reason he would be there. The cabinet maker had realized they were trying to escape.

If they got caught, William didn't care what they did to him. He was strong. He could take the pain but he was terrified of what they would do to punish his wife. *"Fully believing we were caught, I shrank into a corner, turned my face from the door and expected in a moment to be dragged out."*[10]

William knew that if they were caught, he would die a very slow and painful death. Yet his wife would suffer more.

He knew how violent the evil system was. William later wrote how his wife was grateful that she was *"not exposed to many of the worst features of slavery."*

"It's common practice for ladies in the southern states, when angry with their maids, to send them to places established for punishing slaves. They are sent to villains who not only severely flog them as ordered but also make them submit to the greatest indignity."

"Nothing else makes a man's blood boil more than the thought of his wife or young and virtuous daughters becoming prey to these demons."

"Remember that slavery in America is not limited to any particular complexion. There are a lot of white slaves but because the testimony of a slave is not allowed in court, for a white child, after having been kidnapped and sold into slavery in a part of the country where no one knows them, it's almost impossible to ever recover their freedom."

"I have talked with many slaves who said their parents were white and free but they were stolen away from them and sold when quite young. As they could not tell their address, and their parents did not know what had become of their lost little ones, all traces of each other were gone."

"God is just and will not allow the oppressor of the weak to escape unpunished. By persisting in wickedness, they provoke God to pour out His wrath on them. God will avenge the wrongs of His oppressed people. I believe that the same retribution which destroyed Sodom is coming for the slaveholders."[1]

The cabinet maker searched the train, one train car at a time. When he walked through the first-class car, he looked right at Ellen but didn't recognize her. The disguise worked. Still, he kept searching, row by row.

William saw the cabinet maker coming towards him and sunk down in his seat, silently praying for a miracle.

The miracle happened.

Just moments before the cabinet maker reached the train car where William was, suddenly the train horn sounded.

That sound was the last warning before the train left the station, making the cabinet maker realize he had to get off the train.

William's heart started beating again as he saw the cabinet maker leaving.

As the train left the station, William closed his eyes and thanked God.

"God had answered our prayer. Without his kind, special providence we would have never overcome the mountainous difficulties."[12]

They were still in serious danger. Ellen was sitting in a car full of slaveholders. All the other passengers wanted to make conversation with her. How could she stay quiet for long? How could she disguise her soft, female voice? One mistake and she would get caught.

Even worse, she had recognized one of the other passengers. Of all the people that could have happened to sit near her, it was Mr. Cray, who had known her from childhood. Mr. Cray had just seen her yesterday when he visited her master's family for dinner. Now he was sitting nearby and trying to make conversation with her.

Fear gripped her heart until Mr. Cray looked at her and said, *"Good morning, Sir."*

Once again, the disguise was working. If even Mr. Cray couldn't recognize her, maybe she still had a chance.

Ellen sat quietly, pretending she couldn't hear him.

He repeated himself. She looked at him, replied with a quiet *"yes"* and tried to pretend that she was deaf.

Mr. Cray replied with a remark about how nice the morning was. Again, Ellen said nothing. Another passenger remarked about how difficult life was for deaf people. Mr. Cray replied, *"Yes. I won't trouble that fellow any more."*[13]

He began making conversation with the other passengers, as Ellen breathed a sigh of relief. Once again God had answered their prayers.

THE DANGER GROWS

As the train traveled on, the other passengers discussed the three major topics of the day: cotton, slaves, and abolitionists. Ellen smiled, hearing them discuss how much progress the abolitionists had made. While others worried about the future of the nation, Ellen hoped and prayed the abolitionists would be successful.

That night, the train pulled into the station at Savannah. William and Ellen got off and boarded a steamboat headed for Charleston, South Carolina. This time Ellen went straight to her stateroom so none of the other passengers would try to talk to her.

Other passengers noticed that it seemed strange for a person to board a ship and then remain in the stateroom, instead of exploring the ship.

William was prepared for this. He pulled out some towels with a nasty smelling medicine paste and began warming the towels by the stove in the salon. When the other passengers asked about the smell, William explained that his master was ill with a rheumatism. He had to prepare this doctor prescribed treatment, while the master tried to get some rest.

One passenger replied, *"That stinks enough to kill or cure twenty men. Get that out of here."*[14]

William obeyed and was able to spend the evening alone with his wife in their stateroom. The plan was working.

The next morning, Ellen knew she had to blend in by eating breakfast in the dining room. So she boldly walked in and sat down. Since her arm was still *"broken,"* William came over and cut her food for her. This was exactly what they would be doing if they actually were a master and slave traveling together. The only thing that seemed strange to the other passengers was how William was much more attentive to the needs of his master than would typically be expected.

After William had finished taking care of the food, he played the role by leaving the dining car. Meanwhile, Ellen ate her meal with her good hand.

Once again, the other passengers wanted to make conversation with her. They warned her to be really careful when she reached the north. Slaves were known to disappear the moment they were brought to a free state. One passenger told her, *"Watch him like a hawk when you get on to the north. I know several gentlemen who have lost their valuable slaves among them damned cut throat abolitionists."*[15]

Before Ellen could respond, another passenger, who was a well-known slave trader, interrupted. *"Never take a slave north. You won't have them very long once they get across the Mason-Dixon line. They get filled to the brim with damned abolitionist vices and come back to taint all the other slaves. I can already tell that your slave is smart and will definitely run away."*[16]

Ellen smiled, thanked him for the advice and replied that she had no choice. She had to seek treatment in the north for her illness. Besides, she had great confidence in her slave. However, since she wasn't feeling well, she would need to go back to her room. She stayed there the rest of the day with William going in and out of the room to wait on her.

When the ship docked at Charleston, they stayed on board until all the other passengers had left. William carried out the luggage and summoned a horse drawn carriage to take them to the hotel. Ellen hobbled out, appearing very frail.

They were driven to the best hotel in Charleston. Upon arrival, the workers saw how ill Ellen was and helped her hobble into the hotel. She booked one of the best rooms and went to lay down. Once again, William worked on preparing the smelly treatment for her *"illness."*

That night they stuck to the plan, playing their roles very carefully. She ate dinner in the hotel restaurant. William ate dinner in the kitchen with the other servants. The next morning, they checked out of the hotel and went down to buy a ticket to sail by steamboat to Philadelphia.

That's when they found out that the steamboats didn't sail from Georgia in the winter. Plus, the last time they had sailed, a fugitive slave had been caught on board the ship. They would just have to find another route north that wouldn't look suspicious.

Prior to their trip, William had researched how the mail was distributed from the south to the north. He discovered an alternate steamboat route from Savannah, Georgia to Wilmington, North Carolina. This route was still running during the winter months.

Together William and Ellen boldly went down to the ticket office and tried to buy tickets.

The ticket agent was suspicious. He demanded that Ellen sign both of their names on the registry and pay an additional $1 import tax.

Ellen paid the dollar. Then she asked the agent to sign the book for her since her right arm was *"broken."*

The ticket agent refused. That got the attention of other passengers waiting in the ticket office. Everyone turned around to see what Ellen would do. She stood there in silence, with her heart beating furiously.

The answer to their problem walked right through the door.

Back when Ellen had been eating a meal in the dining room on the steamboat, she had met and talked with a young soldier. This soldier came from one of the leading families in Charleston. When he walked into the ticket office and saw her standing there, he stepped forward and vouched for Ellen, saying that he had known her family for years.

The captain of the steamboat also stepped forward and offered to sign the registry for Ellen. Then the captain, not wanting to offend any paying customers, explained that these rules were necessary. *"If they aren't careful, any damned abolitionist might be able to help a lot of slaves escape."*[17]

Once again William and Ellen boarded the ship and continued on their way. They reached Wilmington safely and boarded a train for Richmond, Virginia.

This time there was a different problem.

Ellen rode in a first-class car that had a sitting area with couches. During the trip, she was able to recline on the couch as part of her disguise of being ill. While she was sitting there, an older lady came in and sat down next to her.

When William entered the car, the older lady jumped up and exclaimed, *"That's my slave, Ned!"*

William's heart almost stopped. Had she recognized him? He stood his ground and faced her. She yelled at him, *"Come here you runaway rascal!"*

Ellen said in a voice of authority, *"No. He's mine."*

The other lady looked at both of them and apologized. *"I've never seen two blacks more alike than your boy and my Ned."*[18]

Then the lady began telling a long story about how after her husband had died, many of her slaves began running away.

Ellen patiently listened as William quietly left the car. The lady went on and on, boring the other passengers.

By the time the train reached Richmond, Virginia everyone was so glad to leave to get away from that lady that no one paid any attention to William and Ellen.

They continued on to Washington D.C. and then to Baltimore, Maryland.

Just before Christmas, on December 21, 1848, they arrived at the last port before reaching freedom.

Being this close to freedom made them very nervous. Baltimore was the most dangerous part of the trip because it was watched so closely. Everyone knew that this was the place slaves would try to escape into Pennsylvania. William and Ellen continued playing their roles while fear filled their hearts.

William helped Ellen off the ship and got her onto the first-class train. Then William boarded the economy area and waited for the train to leave.

At this point, they were only hours away from freedom. The train was scheduled to travel all night, reaching Philadelphia in the morning.

Just as the train was preparing to leave, a ticket agent approached William and told him to go to the office because *"It's against the rules for a man to take a slave past here unless he can satisfy them in the office that he has a right to take him along."*

That was not what William wanted to hear. *"The officer then left me standing upon the platform with my anxious heart pounding in my throat. At first, I scarcely knew which way to turn. But it soon occurred to me that the good God, who had been with us thus far, would not forsake us at the eleventh hour. So, with renewed hope I stepped into Ellen's railroad carriage to inform her of the difficulty."*[19]

Ellen jumped when William told her that they had to get off the train. Tears came in her eyes as once again it felt like escape was impossible.

William later described that moment. *"We felt that our very existence was at stake. We must either sink or swim. But as God was our present and mighty helper in this as well as in all former trials, we were able to keep our heads up and press forwards."*

Together they walked into the ticket office as if they had a right to be there. Ellen demanded to know why they were being detained.

The ticket agent explained. *"If any master can prove that a slave escaped on our route, we will have to pay for it. Thus, we cannot let any slave pass here without receiving security that it is all right."*

Ellen replied that they had already bought tickets in Charleston to travel to Philadelphia. *"You have no right to detain us."*

The ticket agent raised his voice and yelled back, *"Right or no right, we won't let you go."*

William and Ellen looked at each other. This was it. If something didn't happen soon, they would get caught. *"We knew that the officers had power to throw us into prison and back to slavery, which we dreaded more than death. Neither of us dared to speak a word for fear of making a mistake."*

"While our hearts cried out to God, who is ever ready to save, the conductor of the train that we had just left stepped in."

The ticket agent asked the conductor if these two passengers had just ridden from Washington, D.C. He replied yes and left.

William: *"Just then the bell rang for the train to leave. As God would have it, the officer all at once said, 'I really don't know what to do. I guess it's all right. Since this gentleman is ill, it's a pity to stop him here.'"*[20]

William and Ellen climbed back on the train and tried to get some rest as the journey continued.

By this time, they had been traveling constantly for four days. The constant stress combined with a lack of sleep was beginning to wear on them.

Eight days had passed since they had had a full night's rest. The four days before they left, they had stayed up all night planning out the trip. Nighttime was the only time that they could see each other and talk, since they were both still working their jobs prior to the trip.

Now on that trip, as the train pulled away from Baltimore, late at night both of them fell into a deep sleep.

When the train came to the Susquehanna River, all of the first-class passengers had to leave the train and board a ferry to cross the river. Ellen got up and walked out with the other passengers.

William was nowhere to be seen. Desperately Ellen looked around for him. Normally at every stop he was always there to help assist her. His constant caring attention had caught the attention of the other passengers who told Ellen how lucky she was to have him. Now she panicked, wondering what had happened to him.

It was dark, cold and rainy as she boarded the ferry alone. All she could do was ask the conductor if anyone had seen her slave.

That was a problem. The conductor was an abolitionist, who was angry at Ellen for being a slaveholder. He refused to help her look for him, insisting that he must have escaped.

Ellen worried. Had William been recognized and arrested? She wanted to stop and look for him, but the ferry was leaving. Besides, she had no way of staying there.

While she was holding the tickets, William had all the money. Just in case there was a pickpocket on board, to protect what little money they had, part of their plan had been to sew the money inside of William's clothes, where no one would look. Now Ellen was all alone, without a dime, but only a faint hope of freedom. She continued on the journey, hoping and praying to find William.

Meanwhile, all this time William was fast asleep in the baggage area where slaves normally rode. He was so sound asleep that when the baggage was transferred to the ferry, they just picked him up and dumped him with the luggage.

After crossing the river, William and the luggage was put back on the train to continue to Philadelphia.

Around that time the conductor and a guard came into the luggage area and woke up William. They said that he should run away. Since his master already thought that he was missing, now was the time to make his escape. Both the conductor and the guard were abolitionists who knew where William could go to connect with the Underground Railroad. They gave him detailed information on whom to contact in Philadelphia. William thanked them, while continuing to keep his cover.

The next morning the train pulled into Philadelphia. William could hardly believe they had made it. He grabbed the luggage, ran to the first-class car and helped his wife. Together they hailed a carriage and drove to the place that the abolitionists had told him to go.

Once they arrived, Ellen burst into tears as all the worry and fear evaporated. They had done the impossible.

For the first time in their lives, on Christmas morning 1848, they were free. They knelt down and *"Poured out our heartfelt gratitude to God for His goodness in enabling us to overcome so many perilous difficulties in escaping out of the jaws of the wicked."*[21]

There they celebrated the miracle. *"Eight days after we had first thought of our plan, we were free from the horrible trammels of slavery and glorifying God who had brought up safely out of a land of bondage."*[22]

They were so grateful to escape and never again have to live under the crushing power of the evil system.

William and Ellen enjoyed their first few weeks in freedom living in the home of some very kind people. The ladies of the house insisted on teaching William and Ellen to read. Then they sent them on to the city of Boston because Philadelphia was not safe for them at all.

However, Boston was a different story. Abolitionists there had worked so fervently that as William later described, *"Public opinion in Massachusetts had become so much opposed to slavery and to kidnapping that it was almost impossible for anyone to take a fugitive slave out of that state. So, we took the advice of our good Philadelphia friends and settled at Boston."*[23]

There they were able to find work and get ahead. William continued working as a carpenter making cabinets and other furniture. Ellen continued working as a talented seamstress.

Their former masters vowed revenge. Bounty hunters were sent to recapture them. So once again they escaped on a boat.

This time they moved to England for twenty years. For the first time they felt truly free and able to raise a family without fear. There they fulfilled their life long dream to have children.

William published a book for future generations to know this story. In the book he shared many shocking historical details.

HIDDEN HISTORY

William wanted people to know something about his family. When he was a child, something had happened in his town.

"I knew a very wealthy gentleman that bought a woman with whom he lived as his wife. They brought up a family of children."

At that time in Georgia, the legal status of children was determined by their mother. William wrote, *"Even if their father is President, if the mother is a slave, the poor child is legally doomed to the same fate."*

"On the father being suddenly killed, it was found that he had not left a will. The family had always heard him say that he had no surviving relatives. Now their protector was gone, knowing the danger to which they were exposed, they were preparing to leave for a free state."

"A villain, hearing of the circumstances, came forward and swore that he was a relative of the deceased. The case was brought before one of those horrible tribunals."

"A verdict was given in favor of the plaintiff whom the community knew had willfully conspired to cheat the family."

"The heartless wretch not only took the ordinary property but actually had the aged and friendless widow and all her fatherless children, brought to the auction stand and sold to the highest bidder."

"The widow had cash enough that her husband had left to purchase the liberty of herself and children but on her attempting to do so, the scoundrel who had robbed them, claimed the money as his property and she had to give it up."

"At the sale, she was brought up first."

"After being vulgarly criticized in the presence of all her distressed family, she was sold to a cotton planter who said he wanted her to watch children for him while their mothers worked in the field."

The evil man Mr. Slator sold the family but kept two of the family members for himself. The oldest son Frank, age 22, and his sister Mary whom William described as *"a very nice girl, a little younger than her brother."*

"Frank and his sister were handcuffed together and confined in prison."

Meanwhile Slator went out and got drunk with the family's money at the local tavern.

Two days later, Slator got a horse and wagon, went to the family's house and stole their valuables. The family had an expensive alcohol and wine collection. Slator took it all.

"He also took with him Frank and Mary as well as all the money from the sale. After treating all his low friends, bystanders and drinking deeply himself, he started (driving) in high glee for his home in South Carolina. But they had not proceeded many miles before Frank and his sister discovered that Slator was too drunk to drive."

"Like most tipsy men, he thought he was all right. He had with him some of the ruined family's best brandy and wine, and being a thirsty soul, he drank till the reins fell from his fingers. When attempting to catch the reins, he tumbled out of the vehicle and was unable to get up."

"Frank and Mary were still handcuffed by one wrist each. They alighted, took the key from the drunken man's pocket, undid the iron bracelets and placed them on Slator as he lay unconscious."

"Frank took from him the large sum of money from the auction as well as the money which Slator had taken from their poor mother."

"Then they dragged him into the woods, tied him to a tree, and left him while they escaped to Savannah, Georgia. The fugitives being white, no one suspected that they were slaves."

"Slator was not able to call anyone to his rescue till late the next day. As there were no railroads in that part of the country at that time, it was not until late the following day that Slator was able to get a group to join him for the chase."

"A person informed Slator that he had met a man and woman driving furiously towards Savannah with the description of those he had lost. So Slator and several slavehunters on horseback started off in full tilt with their bloodhounds in pursuit of Frank and Mary."

"The greatest excitement prevails at a slave hunt. The slaveholders and their hired ruffians take more pleasure in this inhuman pursuit than hunters do in chasing a fox or dog."

"On arriving at Savannah, the hunters found that the fugitives had sold the horses and buggy and embarked as free white persons for New York."

"Slator's disappointment so preyed upon his mind that he went and hanged himself."

"As soon as Frank and Mary were safe, they tried to redeem their good mother but she was gone."

"In due time, Frank learned from his friends in Georgia where his little brother and sister dwelt. So he wrote at once to purchase them but the persons, with whom they lived, would not sell them. After failing in several attempts to buy them, Frank cultivated large whiskers and a moustache, cut off his hair, put on a wig and glasses and went down as a white man to the neighborhood where his sister was."

"After seeing her and his little brother, arrangements were made for them to meet at a place on a Sunday, which they did and left safely."

"I saw Frank myself when he came for the little twins. Though I was then a child, I well remember being highly delighted by hearing him tell how nicely he and Mary had served Slator."

"Frank had so completely disguised his appearance that his little sister did not know him and would not speak until he showed their mother's picture, which melted her to tears for she knew the face."

"Frank and Mary's mother was my wife's dear aunt."[24]

After the Civil War, William and Ellen returned to America, moved to the South and purchased a farm. They offered jobs to freed slaves to help others escape the low paying sharecropping jobs in which many people felt trapped.

They also started a school for freed slaves. Their school was so successful that the Ku Klux Klan burned down their farm as retaliation.

William and Ellen tried buying another farm but were driven out by false accusations from their neighbors. They ended up living with their grown daughter.

Their love lasted a lifetime until Ellen passed at age 65 in 1891. Then William died at age 76 in 1900.

There's another story about William and Ellen Craft that they wanted future generations to know. When they first escaped from slavery, something had happened while they lived in Boston.

They had no idea they were about to make front page headlines. They were just working hard and renting a room at Lewis Hayden's home in Boston.

(To be continued in the Lewis Hayden Story......)

2

Lewis Hayden

"Blessed be the Lord my strength,
who teaches my hands to war and my fingers to fight."
Psalms 144:1 (KJV)

Lewis Hayden
1811-1889
From Lexington, Kentucky

This was going to be a long night in Boston.

Lewis Hayden had barricaded himself in his home with several friends and enough guns and ammo to do some major damage. Word on the street was that bounty hunters were on their way. While Hayden was a fugitive, they were not coming for him. They wanted the two people Hayden was hiding.

The bounty hunters had no idea of the ambush waiting for them.

Hayden and his team were prepared to unleash hell. Hopefully they would be able to persuade the bounty hunters to leave peacefully. Yet if worse came to worse, Hayden had rigged enough gunpowder to blow the whole house. No matter what was about to happen, one thing was certain. There was no way they would be dragged back to slavery.

Lewis Hayden Photo Courtesy of Houghton Library, Harvard
University. Public Domain.

EARLY YEARS

Lewis Hayden had been born under the horrific system of slavery in Lexington, Kentucky. Every day he saw evil hiding in the pulpit. He hated pastors because he was owned by Adam Rankin, Pastor of the Presbyterian Church.

He never dreamed that one day the person who would help him escape from slavery would be a pastor.

Years later Hayden would learn that for every proslavery pastor in America, there were many other abolitionist pastors, risking their lives to run the Underground Railroad. Hayden's master, Adam Rankin, was actually related to John Rankin, the famous abolitionist pastor who operated one of the biggest Underground Railroad stations right on the border of Kentucky and Ohio.

When a desperate mother, pursued by slave catchers, took her chances to run across the thin ice of the Ohio River while holding her baby, she headed for John Rankin's house. Before dashing out onto the thin ice, she grabbed a piece of wood fencing for protection in case she fell through the ice, she could hold onto the wood (stretched across the ice) to keep from going underwater. So the mother ran across the frozen river with her baby in one hand and the piece of wood fencing in the other. She made it safely and lived the rest of her life in freedom.

Hayden would later tell that true story to Harriett Beecher Stowe who wrote it into the novel *Uncle Tom's Cabin.* She could not even print the rescuer John Rankin's name because he would have been brutally punished and his property seized and sold at auction.

At a very young age, Hayden lost both of his parents under tragic circumstances. His father was owned by a different planter. When that planter moved far away, Hayden never saw his father again.

His mother was driven to mental illness by the abuse she suffered.

Years of pain and misery broke down her mind until she began acting strangely. Hayden's last memory of his mother was watching her go into a fit of rage. She tried to kill him when he was too little to protect himself.

He screamed and people intervened just in time. She was taken away to jail. He never saw her again. Hayden had to raise himself and his brothers and sisters.

When Hayden was fourteen, something happened that changed his life forever. The county where he lived had been named Fayette to honor the famous French General Lafayette who had helped America win its independence in the Revolutionary War.

In 1825, Lafayette was invited by President Monroe and Congress to celebrate America's fifty year anniversary of freedom. Lafayette came and spent weeks attending celebrations in many different towns. Everywhere he went, hundreds of Revolutionary War veterans cheered his arrival. Many of them remembered his strong leadership, kindness and generosity when they had served together in the war. Parades were organized in Washington D.C., New York, Boston, Philadelphia, and many other towns he visited.

The town of Lexington, Kentucky also planned to celebrate his arrival with a big parade of veterans, followed by a military escort of active duty soldiers and other distinguished guests.

Like everyone else, Lewis Hayden tried to finish his work in time so he could go watch the parade. However, unlike everyone else, Hayden knew he would have to keep his distance from the crowd. Maybe he could find a place by himself so he wouldn't get in trouble for being at the celebration. Seeing the crowds of people lining the road, Hayden went to the very end of the parade route and climbed up on a fence to watch.

As the parade came, he admired the neatly dressed soldiers with their uniforms looking pressed and perfect. Behind them came General Lafayette riding in an open carriage.

Lafayette greeted the crowd on both sides of the parade route, waving and bowing as he passed.

Hayden couldn't take his eyes off Lafayette. This was the man that everyone was talking about. As Hayden watched him pass by, something happened.

Portrait of Lafayette by C. Schuessele

Lafayette with George Washington during the Revolutionary
War. Artist is Rembrandt Peale (1778-1860)

He described, *"Lafayette was in a barouche drawn by four horses. As he passed the people, he bowed to them on both sides. When he passed me, he bowed to the fence I was on. I looked around and saw no one else on the fence. What did I do but roll right down on the ground, frightened almost to death."*[25]

Something changed in his heart that day. That simple gesture of respect from his hero, touched him deeply. Maybe there was more to life than the constant abuse Hayden had endured. Maybe he was worth more than people wanted him to know. Maybe there was a better life outside the only life he had ever known.

Hayden later described how that brief moment transformed him. *"Lafayette was the most famous man I had ever heard of. You can image how I felt as a slave boy to be favored with his recognition. From that day forward, I allowed nothing to stand between me and my freedom."*[26]

Before freedom came, things changed for the worse. Hayden's master got in trouble with the Presbyterian denomination. They thought he was too strict. They didn't like how he refused to allow hymns to be sung in church and were deeply offended by how he had criticized other ministers involved in a local revival. He was kicked out of the denomination. So he decided to move back to Pennsylvania where he was from.

Pennsylvania was a free state. For a brief moment, Hayden had a glimmer of hope. But that hope would be shattered when he realized the master's actual plans were to sell all of his slaves to finance his move.

Hayden felt the shame of being traded for a wagon and pair of horses. Meanwhile, his brothers and sisters were sold at public auction.

That hurt Hayden deeply. *"I had hoped that he would take me with him where I should get free. How I looked at those horses with strange feelings, thinking that I had been sold for them."*[27]

Hayden's new master was a merchant who traveled around the country selling handmade clocks. Living on the road, gave Hayden the chance to see more of the world outside his hometown.

Hayden absorbed everything he could, paying attention to conversations he heard in places where they stayed on their journeys. He also taught himself to read and began absorbing the Bible.

Then he fell in love. Her name was Esther Harvey and she was owned by a local businessman. Hayden married her. Soon they had a son.

More trouble came. His wife's master's business was in trouble. When he went bankrupt, everything he owned was sold to pay the debts.

U.S. Senator Henry Clay

Hayden's wife and child were sold to Henry Clay, the Kentucky Senator. That weighed heavily on Hayden's mind. What could he do?

Hayden knew that Henry Clay had powerful friends in Washington. Clay's circle of influence was too powerful for Hayden to have any chance against him.

Hayden still did everything he could to protect his wife and child only to watch them ripped from his hands. Only months after purchasing them, Henry Clay decided to resell them.

Hayden never saw them again. That hurt more than anything else. Hayden patiently waited for years until the time came to get revenge.

The time came when Henry Clay ran for President. In the 1844 election, Clay faced off against James Polk. Drawing upon years of political favors, he was favored to win the Presidency. The newspapers backed Clay's candidacy, writing glowing articles about how wonderful he was. One paper even proclaimed him as a friend to black people.

Clay had a great reputation in Washington until Hayden took him down.

Hayden wrote to the newspaper and shredded Clay's reputation by exposing his dark side. Describing how cruel Clay had been behind closed doors, Hayden wrote, *"My family is not the only one that Henry Clay has destroyed. May God save us all from such a friend!"*

Then reminding everyone how someday Clay would have to stand before God to answer for his deeds, Hayden wrote how on Judgement Day, *"Other broken hearts besides mine and my wife's will rise up in judgment against him."*[28]

This became a major news story, which the political opposition used to its advantage to destroy Clay's reputation in the election.

Henry Clay was furious at this public humiliation. Denying all the facts, he claimed that he had never owned Hayden's family. Then he tried to patch up his tarnished reputation by attacking Hayden as a *"Drunken, worthless person."*[29]

It was too late. No one believed him. Clay would win almost half the popular vote, only to lose the presidential election to James Polk.

That wouldn't be the only victory Hayden won against Clay. But first Hayden had to gain his own freedom.

By this time, he had fallen in love again and started a new family.

For years he had been looking for the way out.

Living in Lexington, left him with few options for escape. All the ways to enter and exit the city were closely watched. The roads were patrolled with heavily armed law enforcement. Escape was just too risky. One wrong move and he would be captured, punished, and sold somewhere he would never see his new wife and son again. That thought was just too painful.

He also had a new job, working as a waiter in the local hotel. This job became his way out. While he still had to turn over most of his wages to his owner, he made enough tips to save some money. Hayden began secretly saving up money for the day that opportunity would knock at his door. It would come much sooner than he expected.

FREEDOM COMES

Hayden had a friend in the town named Delilah Webster. She had started out as a school teacher only to realize that no matter how hard she worked, she would never be paid fairly.

Male teachers would always be paid much more for the same work. It wasn't fair, still she found a way to beat the system.

By quitting her teaching job to launch her own school, she was able to do what she loved and make a decent living. Her school was very successful, providing her with a much better steady income than she had previously made as a teacher.

This was also her cover for working on the Underground Railroad (UGRR). Through those connections, she met Calvin Fairbanks, who gave Hayden the way out.

Fairbanks was a pastor by day and conductor on the UGRR at night. Every penny he had went to helping people escape.

Being a pastor was how Fairbanks could travel frequently to and from the South, taking groups with him without too many people asking questions. Knowing all the best escape routes, Fairbanks was highly skilled at moving people without detection.

Yet no matter how many successful missions he completed, he was always just one mistake away from getting caught and brutally punished. This was a very dangerous job. Every step had to be carefully planned because anyone could turn him in at any time. That was a risk he was willing to take to give freedom to total strangers.

Fairbanks had been asked to travel to Lexington to rescue the wife of a former slave named Gilson Berry.

While every step had been carefully planned, nothing went as planned.

Fairbanks arrived in Lexington only to find that Berry's wife was nowhere to be found. Had the wrong people been tipped off?

Trying to find her, Fairbanks ran out of money. It was time to go home before anyone figured out who he really was. Maybe he could help someone else instead. Then this trip wouldn't be for nothing. So Fairbanks went to Delilah to ask about options. She introduced him to Lewis Hayden, suggesting there was a different way to make this trip successful.

By this time, Hayden had saved up enough money to escape.

Fairbanks met with Hayden to figure out the right strategy. They developed a clever plan. Fairbanks would rent a carriage with Hayden's money. Then Fairbanks and Delilah would travel north in the carriage. Hidden inside the carriage would be Hayden, his wife Harriet and their son Joseph.

It was a brilliant plan with a lot of risks. Traveling north required successfully passing through several road checkpoints.

One mistake and there would be brutal consequences. But Fairbanks knew that traveling with a lady would make it less likely for the carriage to be searched.

Just a few days later at 5:00pm on a Saturday evening, Delilah was seen leaving the town in a carriage with Fairbanks. Hidden inside was the Hayden family. Just in case anyone looked closely at the carriage, the Hayden family had covered their faces in flour to appear lighter skinned.

Just when they had gotten onto the main road, they realized that one of the rented horses was very sick. Too sick to travel very far. There was no other choice but to stop at a tavern and rent another horse.

The good thing was that they were getting closer to the border of Kentucky and Ohio. They continued traveling very carefully. Once they safely made it onto the ferry to cross the Ohio River, they all breathed a sigh of relief.

When they reached Ohio, Fairbanks took them directly to the city of Ripley where John Rankin lived.

This town had become such a successful UGRR operation that the slavehunters referred to it as a *"black, dirty, abolition hole."*[30]

Rankin helped transfer the Hayden family further north. Within days they had made it safely to Canada.

Meanwhile, back in Lexington things were heating up. The Hayden family had been reported missing. The hunt for them began.

The landlord at the boardinghouse went into Delilah's room, looked through all her stuff and found letters written between Fairbanks and Delilah. These letters revealed they had been working together in the escape.

When Fairbanks and Delilah returned home and turned in the rental carriage, they were arrested. Both of them were put on trial and found guilty. Fairbanks was sentenced to fifteen years of hard labor.

Delilah was sentenced to two years in prison. She would become the only female prisoner in the Kentucky state prison, gaining the sympathy of many people, who petitioned the governor to pardon her. She was released after serving only several weeks of the sentence.

Meanwhile, Pastor Fairbanks suffered in prison for years. It was a brutal life. Prisoners were required to earn their keep by performing heavy manual labor. Fairbanks was forced to work like a slave in the prison, suffering frequent beatings by the guards and all kinds of abuse.

Still Fairbanks continued pastoring inside the prison, ministering to a group of fifty prisoners. Fairbanks brought the light of the Gospel into a very dark place.

Four long years passed before Fairbanks would be rescued by Hayden. During that time, Hayden worked and saved up money. When he finally had enough funds, Hayden negotiated a deal to buy freedom for Fairbanks. The deal was Hayden paid his former master $650 in damages. In return, the former master successfully petitioned Kentucky's Governor to release Fairbanks.

The plan worked.

Then as soon as Fairbanks was released, he went right back to running the Underground Railroad. Too many people were suffering under the evil system. Fairbanks had a soft heart and couldn't enjoy his freedom while others continued to suffer.

Once again, Fairbanks was caught helping people escape. This time he suffered in prison for fifteen years. Lewis Hayden did everything possible to help him but the brutal system showed no mercy. Fairbanks suffered in prison for fifteen years until the Civil War came.

Meanwhile, Lewis Hayden was starting a new life with the freedom and safety he had always dreamed about.

Freedom was intoxicating. The more he lived it, the more he realized his rights. Finally he could say everything he had been thinking during all the years he suffered in silence.

Hayden wrote a letter to his former masters, gloating about how wonderful it was *"to try freedom and how it will seem to be my own master."*[81]

The letter upset them but there was nothing they could do about it. Hayden was safe in Canada where they couldn't touch him.

The Hayden family settled into their new life, working hard and getting involved in the local community.

Yet it didn't feel like where they were supposed to be. Within months they made the decision to move back to America, settling in Detroit. There they got involved in the local African Methodist Episcopal Church (AME), helping the pastor raise funds for a new building.

By then the story of Hayden's escape had become national news. Everyone was talking about the laws that had imprisoned Fairbanks and Delilah. Hayden was invited to make public appearances, telling his story to various abolitionist groups.

Boston area political activists hoped that Hayden's story would move the heart of the nation towards freedom.

Hayden and his Pastor Brown, traveled to Boston and appeared at several different events, raising funds to pay for the new church building back in Detroit. Their trip was very successful. Boston welcomed them with open arms, as it was the headquarters for the abolitionist movement.

For Hayden, the highlight of the trip was getting to attend his first antislavery convention. It felt like a dream, seeing so many people that hated slavery as much as he did and were organizing to vigorously oppose it. *"I forgot myself and felt that I was in paradise."*[32]

Here was a well organized network of people, including several pastors running the Underground Railroad. Hayden was asked to speak at the convention. Before he took the podium, it was announced that if any slave catchers came to Boston and tried to touch Hayden, the city was prepared to forcibly protect him.

After listening to Hayden share his testimony before the convention, people realized that he was a gifted public speaker who could do much for their cause.

William Lloyd Garrison, who was leading the American Anti-Slavery Society (AAS), told other leaders that Hayden *"is a rare young man"* who *"needs to be with us more."*[33]

Garrison encouraged Hayden to move to Boston where there was one of the broadest bases of support in the country.

After the convention, Hayden was asked to become a paid public speaker for the AAS. They offered a salary of about $600 and complete flexibility to travel America and turn the tide of public opinion.

Hayden accepted and soon left for the road. A partner from the AAS traveled with him as a co-speaker. Hayden started the meetings by sharing his testimony, then the other speaker, Dr. Darwin Hudson, shared the goals of the AAS and invited people to join their cause.

The speaking tour was a big success. Everywhere they went, large crowds turned out to see them. Hearts were moved. Many new volunteers were recruited. The abolitionist movement became more successful than ever.

Then the abolitionist movement split right down the middle.

William Lloyd Garrison was too stubborn to listen to his team. He was critical of everything that was not exactly how he thought it should be.

He pushed for extreme measures that failed to accomplish anything and only turned people against the cause.

Garrison believed that all government was sinful. Even voting itself was sinful. True Christians could not vote or run for political office, because they should have nothing to do with the evil world, but limit themselves to trying to change the nation with moral arguments.

Words only. No physical action. Garrison also condemned any use of force to protect fugitive slaves from pursuers. Garrison wrote from the comfort of his home, never understanding how dangerous the world was. He ignored the very real danger faced by many other people.

Garrison caused many abolitionists to stop voting, which only helped elect more proslavery candidates. The wrong side grew stronger while abolitionists pleaded with Garrison to see the problems with his philosophy.

Garrison refused to understand how he was actually helping to elect proslavery candidates by keeping abolitionists from the polls.

The AAS, which began as a powerful organization focused on fighting slavery, got side tracked into small political differences.

This dispute grew worse and worse until one of the Lane Rebels, Henry Stanton, publicly confronted Garrison.

At one of the largest abolitionist conventions in Massachusetts, Stanton stood up and publicly demanded answers from Garrison.

"Do you or do you not believe it's a sin to go to the polls?"

Garrison responded with a cocky grin. *"Sin for me."*[34]

Stanton rolled his eyes. What good was that? Couldn't he see that this was ripping the AAS apart? Stanton devoted his efforts to getting as many people to vote as possible, while Garrison continued getting in the way.

Thinking that voting was sinful continued keeping abolitionists from the polls for many years until 1856 when Lincoln addressed it in his speech. *"Do not mistake that the ballot is stronger than the bullet."*

"Therefore let the legions of slavery use bullets. But let us wait patiently until November and fire ballots at them in return. By that peaceful policy we will ultimately win."[35]

Hayden agreed. Believing that every potential tool should be used, he insisted that everyone had to get out and vote for antislavery candidates. He also understood the need to physically intervene if anyone tried to recapture fugitive slaves.

Because Hayden stood his ground, refusing to preach Garrison's extreme views, after several months of his successful speaking tour, he was fired by the AAS. Hayden graciously left the organization, saying he wished he could have done more for them.

He returned home to Detroit, then moved his family to Boston where the next chapter of his life began.

Hayden became a successful businessman, opening a used clothing store and boardinghouse. This was the perfect cover for his real job of running a safe house on the Underground Railroad. Guests hiding in his home were clothed from the store and fed from the boardinghouse. Plus running the boardinghouse enabled him to purchase large quantities of food without anyone getting suspicious.

This was the life Hayden had always wanted. He was living with his family in freedom, making a good living and helping others escape.

Things were going well until everything changed in 1850.

For years, thousands of people had escaped on the Underground Railroad. They were helped along by total strangers who fed, hid, and passed them along until they reached the safety of the North.

Yet the proslavery power was determined to destroy this network. Too many bounty hunters were being hindered by ordinary armed citizens.

Several free states had even dared to pass laws protecting the rights of fugitive slaves.

FIGHTING THE
FUGITIVE SLAVE LAW

So the proslavery power decided that the only recourse they had was to get a new law passed which would go way beyond any previous law in protecting slavery.

The Compromise of 1850, a Fugitive Slave Law, was proposed in Congress. Henry Clay promoted it as the only way to save the Union.

This law gave slave catchers the ability to hunt fugitives in free states and drag them back to bondage.

The right of trial by jury was thrown out the window. Bounty hunters would be able to go into any free state and drag anyone off the street that they claimed was a fugitive. The only evidence necessary was a sworn affidavit. Fugitives had no access to a jury trial and could not even testify in their own defense. Their case could only be heard by a special commissioner who would be financially rewarded if he returned them to slavery.

The worst part of the law was that it required the local towns-people to help the bounty hunters do their dirty work. Anyone who refused to help could be brutally punished with a massive fine of $1,000 which would cost them their house, farm and just about everything they owned.

When this law was proposed in Congress, it met a firestorm of op-position. Abolitionist Senator John P. Hale fought back with speeches on the unconstitutionality of it.

Yet no matter how hard Senator Hale fought, he could not stop the proslavery majority from passing the Fugitive Slave Law. It was signed into law by President Millard Fillmore.

While the proslavery majority thought this would put an end to the conflict over slavery, it actually backfired in a big way.

People knew the Bible well enough to know that God hated slavery. They talked about God's command in Deuteronomy 23:15: *"Thou shalt not return a fugitive slave to his master."*

News quickly spread across the nation that no fugitive slave would be safe in America any more. Meetings were held in African American communities to discuss options. For many the only solution was to move to Canada. Many African American families packed up and left for safety in Canada. Meanwhile, families that stayed behind organized into armed resistance.

The city of Boston came together to fight this law.

On September 30, 1850, Lewis Hayden served as Chairman of a meeting at a church packed with people willing to fight.

Hayden stood up and called for people to come together in armed resistance with *"ways and means for the protection of those in Boston likely to be seized by the prowling man-thief."*[36]

Then they issued a proclamation that they were invoking their God given rights and would *"defend ourselves and each other in resisting this God-defying and inhuman law at any and every sacrifice."*[37]

The African American community in Boston made it very clear through a written resolution that no law would be able to stop them from protecting their own. *"God willed us free. Man willed us slaves. God's will be done. We pledge ourselves to resist unto death any attempt upon our liberties."*[38]

A few days later on October 4, 1850, the black community of Boston met again and resolved to defend *"the soil of Bunker Hill, Concord and Lexington,"* where the American Revolution had begun.

Hayden led the meeting and listened intently as they figured out the next steps.

They talked about the best options for civil disobedience. Garrison was at the meeting and told them to avoid using physical violence. Just be peaceful.

The rest of the people knew better.

The black community ignored Garrison's advice and decided that it was better to die fighting and *"rot beneath the soil than to be true to church and state while we are false (disobedient) to God."*[39]

They issued another proclamation demanding that law enforcement *"obey God rather than the devil by letting the oppressed go free (Isaiah 58:6)."*

They warned people to be careful when walking the streets and be prepared to fight if anyone tried to kidnap them. Recognizing the *"danger"* caused by the *"bribes"* paid to judges, they told law enforcement that *"any commissioner who would deliver up a fugitive"* to a bounty hunter was no better than Judas who gave up *"Jesus to his prosecutors."*[40]

Boston resident Joseph Smith, reminded them of Jeremiah 8:11 which warns against calling for peace when there is no peace. He encouraged every black family to buy a Colt's revolver for protection against slave catchers saying, *"If liberty is not worth fighting for, it is not worth having."*[41]

Another member of the black community, Robert Johnson, asked all the ladies working in local hotels to keep an eye out for bounty hunters and warn the team if any arrived.

They also formed the Vigilance Committee: a well organized group of heavily armed black and white men, prepared to defend any fugitive in the city from being kidnapped.

They issued a public statement warning slave catchers that it would be dangerous to come to Boston.

"Believing that resistance to tyrants is obedience to God, we are resolved to organize. We are ready to obey God rather than the devil, resist the law, rescue and protect the slave and wipe out the foul stain of this law inflicted by Daniel Webster."[42]

(Webster was the U.S. Senator from Boston who had once been an abolitionist. When he switched sides to support the 1850 Fugitive Slave Bill, that infuriated his constituents. They felt betrayed. So they voted Webster out and Boston sent the abolitionist Charles Sumner to Congress instead.)

As one of the directors of the Boston Vigilance Committee, Hayden was actively involved in armed resistance to the law.

The Vigilance Committee formed a guard to watch the city of Boston for any bounty hunters. They were barely just in time.

Some of the very first fugitives hunted down under this law were William and Ellen Craft. Their former master was tipped off that they were living openly in Boston at Lewis Hayden's house.

Bounty hunters, John Knight and Willis Hughes were sent to find them. What happened next would make front page headlines across the nation.

On Saturday October 19, 1850, the bounty hunters arrived in Boston and checked into a hotel. It was the weekend. All government offices were closed. Knowing they would have to wait until Monday to file for a warrant to arrest the Crafts, they relaxed, had drinks and got comfortable.

They had no idea they were being closely watched.

A newspaper in Georgia had published the plans of the former master of William and Ellen Craft, who had vowed to recapture them.

Abolitionists in the South had read the newspaper and warned abolitionists in Boston that Knight and Hughes were coming. From the moment they set foot in Boston, they were closely followed.

Everywhere the bounty hunters went, they were booed and threatened. Men threw stones at them. Ladies called them dirty rotten thieves. Slowly they realized that the city of Boston was serious when they had vowed that no fugitive could ever be taken there. The Vigilance Committee was working night and day to organize different groups to fight back.

On Monday morning, Knight and Hughes went to the courthouse to file paperwork requesting a warrant to be issued for the arrest of the Crafts.

Boston authorities responded by arresting Knight and Hughes for attempted kidnapping. They posted bail and were released.

Lawyers from the Vigilance Committee filed a lawsuit against them claiming that they were violating the civil rights of the Crafts.

Knight and Hughes were arrested again.

Once again, they posted bail and were released. But this time a crowd of several hundred had gathered around the courthouse. Someone was standing on a box, urging everyone to arm themselves and murder the slave catchers. The bounty hunters carefully made their way through the crowd and into a horse drawn carriage waiting for them. Scared for their lives, they drove off at a high rate of speed.

They were promptly arrested for speeding. This time their bail was set at $20,000. Yet again, they posted bail and were released. Then they had to be escorted to their hotel under armed guard because the crowd outside the courthouse was threatening to tar and feather them.

The *American Beacon* newspaper reported, *"Much excitement prevails among the negro population. The courthouse has been surrounded by them all morning. They are determined to resist even to the shedding of blood any attempt at carrying back to slavery their colored brethren. The impression is that serious consequences will follow if an attempt be made to arrest."*[43]

Meanwhile, Hayden was preparing his home for a violent confrontation.

William and Ellen Craft had been renting a room in Hayden's home ever since they had escaped from slavery. They paid for their room and board with William working as a carpenter and Ellen as a seamstress.

When news spread through the city that the bounty hunters were coming, many people visited the Hayden home and offered to help. William Lloyd Garrison the pacifist came by with the famous British abolitionist George Thompson and was impressed to see how prepared they were.

"The windows were barricaded. The doors, double locked and barred. Around a table covered with loaded weapons were Lewis Hayden, his young son and a group of brave colored men, armed to the teeth, ready for the impending death struggle with the U.S. Marshal and his armed posse."[44]

Another friend, Frederick Douglas published this notice in his newspaper. *"Mr. Craft is armed and resolved to stand his ground. Blood may flow in the streets of Boston."*[45]

This was a fight to the death.

Hayden and Craft had sent both of their wives to stay at the home of their friend Pastor Theodore Parker.

Then they worked together on rigging gunpowder in Hayden's basement. If the confrontation turned into a brutal fight, Hayden and Craft would set off the gunpowder, blowing the whole house, knowing that their wives were safe somewhere else.

Then Hayden sent word to the bounty hunters that he was waiting for them. He promised that the moment they set foot on his property, he would walk out on his front porch with a lighted torch and set off the gunpowder.

The bounty hunters did some recon work. They realized that not only was Hayden's home heavily fortified, but the entire street was heavily armed and well prepared for a major confrontation. No one could even walk down that street without being watched by many eyes.

Crowds gathered around the hotel where the bounty hunters were staying and kept an all night vigil. They chanted. They threatened, booed and hissed. They told the bounty hunters to go home and never come back.

No one in the hotel was able to sleep that night.

The next day, Pastor Parker visited the bounty hunters at their hotel and warned them to leave because *"They were not safe in Boston another night."*[46]

The bounty hunters were also warned by local law enforcement that if they broke down the door to Lewis Hayden's home, they would be arrested for breaking and entering.

The violent confrontation never came.

The bounty hunters gave up and snuck out of the city, trying to avoid all the people watching their every move. They returned home and reported back that serving the warrants was impossible.

William and Ellen's former masters wrote directly to President Fillmore, demanding that the Fugitive Slave Law (FSL) be enforced by the federal government.

By this time former Senator Daniel Webster had been appointed Secretary of State. He wrote to President Millard Fillmore complaining of the *"clumsy"* law enforcement in Boston. He recommended that the federal government respond quickly to crush any rebellion. Webster himself organized a town hall meeting to promote the idea of enforcing the FSL.

President Fillmore replied that he didn't see the need to send troops to Boston yet, but he would if it became necessary.

It would quickly become necessary.

William and Ellen Craft were put on the first ship to England where they were able to live in peace until peace returned to America at the end of the Civil War and they returned home.

But before that happened, Boston continued protecting their residents.

More slaveowners sent bounty hunters to Boston to capture their fugitives. Again the city resisted. Fugitives were smuggled out of the city and sent to Canada.

Slaveowners became frustrated with how impossible it seemed to capture anyone in Boston.

That was about to change.

On February 15, 1851, in Boston, U.S. Marshals arrested fugitive slave Shadrach Minkins at the restaurant where he worked. Shadrach was taken to the courthouse and put in jail to wait until he would appear before the commissioner. Guards were posted outside the courthouse in case anyone tried to interfere.

They were barely just in time. Within minutes, a crowd had gathered outside the courthouse to demand the release of Shadrach.

Lewis Hayden was leading the crowd. The moment they heard what had happened, Hayden and his friends had rushed down to the courthouse. Among them were lawyers from the Vigilance Committee, which promptly filed affidavits on Shadrach's behalf.

About an hour later, the hearing was held. The Vigilance lawyers requested more time to prepare a defense for Shadrach. The judge complied, postponing the hearing for a few days.

After the court adjourned and everyone began to leave the courtroom, one black man was overhead telling Shadrach, *"Don't worry, we'll stand by you until death."*[47]

Meanwhile, another one of the Vigilance Committee members, Joseph Hayes, told the crowd to stay close by and just move from the courtroom to the hallway.

Another black man, armed with a knife, replied he was ready.

Another man boldly proclaimed, *"I'll spill the last drop of blood I have before he shall be carried out of the courthouse."*[48]

The U.S. Marshals were getting nervous. They could hear the crowd discussing how ready they were for a fight. After the crowd had left the courtroom, the Marshals closed and locked the courtroom door, while they waited for the last remaining attorneys and news reporters to gather their things to leave.

When they were finally ready, officer Calvin Hutchins carefully opened the courtroom door.

That was what the mob outside had been waiting for. The moment the door opened a crack, they forced it wide open. Rushing into the courtroom, the mob took control. Shadrach was quickly picked up and carried out by several men.

The marshals tried to resist only to be completely overpowered. Shadrach was violently rescued from the courthouse.

Lewis Hayden was seen leading the mob with Shadrach towards his house. Since Hayden's house was the first place that law enforcement would look for Shadrach, they hid him in a widow's house a few doors down from Hayden.

That night Shadrach was driven out of town where he was passed along to Canada.

When he reached Canada, Shadrach was so overwhelmed with emotion that he fell to his knees and thanked God for freedom in such a powerful way that those watching him were moved to tears.

Meanwhile, Hayden made his way back home, staying at the house of Joseph Lovejoy (brother to Owen Lovejoy).

Everything had happened so fast that it took a little while for law enforcement to catch up. Once they realized that Shadrach was gone, they knew there was no way to recapture him. Boston was too strong.

News spread rapidly across the nation. Front page headlines proclaimed: *"KIDNAPPERS DISAPPOINTED."*[49]

Southern newspapers complained as the nation divided on the issue. On the floor of Congress, Senator Henry Clay was *"shocked and distressed by forcible resistance to a law."*

Demanding that President Fillmore crack down on lawbreakers, Clay noted, *"That mob was pushed forward by people who possess no part in our political system. Shall the government of whites be yielded to the government of blacks? Punish this immediately and maintain the law!"*[50]

Senator John P. Hale was quickly on his feet protesting. *"King George III tried to do the same thing in Boston. He sent his royal army there and they enforced the law by shooting the citizens (in the Boston Massacre). That is not the government we have. Boston will not allow that to happen again."*[51]

That infuriated Senator (and later Confederate President) Jefferson Davis who jumped up to add: *"I never thought the mob could have the power to release a fugitive. Opposition has gone further than I expected."*

"If mobs can rule and the law is dead in Boston then the people are unworthy of the government they inherited."[52]

Proslavery forces moved quickly to crush this rebellion. Secretary of State Daniel Webster met with President Fillmore to discuss their options.

Webster recommended, *"What we need is the conviction and punishment of some of the rescuers. Then it will be as easy to arrest a fugitive slave in Boston as it is to arrest any other person."*[53]

President Fillmore agreed and ordered swift prosecutions *"against all persons who have made themselves aides or abettors in this flagitious offense."*[54]

Ordering military forces in the Boston area to be on alert, he promised to send the full force of the military to crush any future riots and overwhelm any defiant city officials.

Lewis Hayden was quickly arrested. When the officers went looking for him, they found him at the offices of the American Anti-Slavery Association.

Hayden was right in the middle of helping a fugitive mother and child, when the officers knocked at the door. Acting quickly to protect others, Hayden walked out the door and allowed them to cuff him, while the mother and child were hidden. They escaped while Hayden was busy being arrested and posting bail.

Hayden was put on trial for violating the Fugitive Slave Law. Ironically, he was never charged with being a runaway slave himself, because prosecutors knew they could never get that conviction in Boston. However, since the entire jury was required to swear allegiance to the FSL, prosecutors knew they would be able to get a conviction under it.

They were wrong. The trial resulted in a hung jury. While most of the men on the jury had been pressured into voting for a conviction, one man had stood for justice and voted for not guilty.

Years later it would be revealed that the one juror who saved Hayden from prison had also been involved in helping Shadrach escape. Francis Bigelow had been the blacksmith who drove Shadrach out of the city and on to the next station on the UGRR.[55]

The way it happened would later be described by Bigelow's wife Ann:

"Shadrach was still holding the carving knife in one hand, working as a waiter in a hotel on Court Street, when he was arrested by his pretend master. He was hurried at once to the courthouse to be tried."

"On the alarm being given, the courthouse was filled with a crowd of black and white men, who moved forward in a body, surrounded Shadrach and carried him out. No one except Lewis Hayden knew him from any of the other colored men."

"He went out with the rest and was soon lost in the crowd. He and Hayden coolly walked off toward East Cambridge, keeping sight of each other on opposite sides of the street. Here they stopped at the house of Rev J.C. Lovejoy. Then left in a carriage driven by a Mr. Smith."

"They arrived at Concord at 3AM Sunday morning, driving into Mr. Bigelow's yard. Mr. Bigelow, hearing the carriage, opened the door and let in the poor fugitive, though the penalty was a thousand dollars and six months imprisonment for aiding and abetting a fugitive to escape. The blinds of the house were at once shut and the widows darkened. Breakfast was prepared."

"Shadrach was so fatigued with loss of sleep and anxiety, that he could hardly keep awake while eating. As soon as he was refreshed, Mr. Bigelow, in a wagon hired for the purpose, drove him to the house of Dr. Drake in Leominster, another station on the UGRR. From there he was carried to Fitchburg and thence by rail to Canada. Meanwhile, Mr. Hayden and Mr. Smith drove leisurely to Sudbury. There they visited friends, went to church and after a good dinner, returned unhindered to Boston."

"When the trials were on for the rescuers of Shadrach, there was some difficulty in selecting a jury. Mr. Bigelow was drawn once and rejected, but afterwards by some quibble of law, he was again chosen and sat in the case. The rescuers were all cleared by the disagreement of the jury. Mr. Bigelow being the one who stood out."[56]

Years later, Hayden's lawyer Richard Henry Dana was approached by a total stranger who told Dana his side of the story.

"I was a member of the jury. I've never seen two men more worried than you and Mr. Hale worried about their client. There was never any danger of your client being convicted."

Dana: "Why not?"

Jury member: "Because I was the man who took Shadrach at the door of the courthouse and took him to a place of safety in Concord."

"Then from the beginning of the trial, I knew there was never any danger of the jury convicting those men while I was on the jury."[57]

Several other people involved in Shadrach's rescue would also be arrested and put on trial, but none would be convicted. Boston would remain defiant, vowing that no one would be taken in their city.

President Fillmore kept his promise to crack down. When the next fugitive was arrested in Boston, three hundred soldiers were sent to maintain law and order.

Seventeen year old Thomas Sims had escaped from slavery in Georgia by hiding on a boat until he reached Boston. He enjoyed freedom for a while and found a job. Then his former master tracked him down and caught him working at a restaurant.

Just like Shadrach, he was taken to the courthouse. Once again the alarm was sounded. The mob gathered outside to rescue him.

This time they could not get in. The courthouse was too heavily barricaded and guarded by too many soldiers. Sims was sent back to Georgia, but it was only a matter of time until he was able to escape again and make his way back to Boston.

The next fugitive caught in Boston was Anthony Burns. He was arrested while walking down the street in Boston. He was also put in jail at the courthouse.

Thousands of people gathered outside the courthouse to protest while hundreds of soldiers guarded it.

Quickly the tension exploded into a full scale riot as protestors stormed the courthouse and tried to rescue Burns.

This was a well planned attack organized by the Vigilance Committee and led by Hayden. They waited until nightfall, then began by extinguishing the street lights. A log was used as a battering ram to break down the courthouse doors.

Their brave rescue attempt failed. Once they got inside they were quickly overwhelmed by law enforcement.

President Franklin Pierce had made sure to send enough officers and soldiers to stop any rescue.

Anthony Burns was sent back to slavery. As he was dragged out of Boston in chains, thousands of people lined the streets to boo and hiss at law enforcement. They vowed to continue resisting any future attempts to enforce the FSL.

Seeing the real life consequences of this evil law shifted public opinion. People who had been moderate voters began to change their political positions.

As someone who lived during this time, Amos Lawrence, described, *"We went to bed one night as calm moderate voters and woke up as crazy, insane abolitionists."*[58]

The city of Boston would not rest until they had rescued Burns from slavery. Seeing no other option, they raised enough money to purchase his freedom. He would be the last fugitive arrested in Boston as the country slid into Civil War.

Anthony Burns would live the rest of his life in freedom. Yet it would cost him something very precious to him. Even though, when he was a slave, he had also been a pastor ministering to other slaves, his home church published a notice in the newspaper excommunicating him for refusing to return to bondage.

So he wrote a letter, teaching the church the truth.

Burns wrote, *"You have thrust me out of your church fellowship. So be it. You cannot exclude me from Heaven nor hinder my daily fellowship with God."*

"God made me a man—not a slave and gave me the right to myself. No man had any right to steal me. The manstealer who stole me committed an outrage on God's law."

"You accuse me in that escaping I disobeyed God's law. No! That law which God wrote on the table of my heart, inspiring the love of freedom, I obeyed and by the good hand of my God, I walked out of the house of bondage."

"I disobeyed no law of God revealed in the Bible. I read in 1Corinthians 7:21: 'If you may be free, use it.' Deuteronomy 25:15-16 implies my right to flee and bars any from delivering me again to my professed master."

"I said I was stolen. God's Word declares, 'He that steals a man and sells him...he shall be surely put to death (Exodus 21:16).'"

"Why did you not execute God's law on the man who stole me?"

Then he pointed at the Bible and wondered why the church didn't know it.

"How is it that you trample down God's law against the oppressor and wrest it to condemn me, the innocent and oppressed?"

"Have you forgotten that the New Testament classes 'manstealers' with 'murders of fathers and murders of mothers? (1 Timothy 1:9-10)."[59]

Meanwhile, Hayden was fighting another battle to end segregation. When Hayden and his wife traveled from Boston to Vermont, like other passengers, they purchased first class tickets and boarded the train. They completed the journey from Boston to Providence, Rhode Island, then changed trains.

That's when the trouble started. When they boarded the new train, the conductor would not allow them to sit in the first class car.

Hayden protested. Hadn't they paid for first class tickets?

The conductor refused. Adding insult to injury, the conductor remarked that even if they had bought first class tickets in Boston, no one in Providence would sell them those kind of tickets.

Hayden and his wife stood their ground. Refusing to ride in the second class car, instead they got a hotel room for the night.

The next morning they reboarded their previous train, which had allowed them to ride first class. Then they returned to Boston.

Back home in Boston, Hayden confronted the railroad employees about how he had not been able to use the first class tickets he had purchased.

The railroad employees gave them a full refund and issued new tickets free of charge for the Haydens to complete their trip to Vermont.

Yet when the Haydens boarded the train again, they were surprised to see how the railroad was still enforcing segregation in a different way. One entire first class railroad car had been added to the train just for them. They rode by themselves for the rest of the journey.

This was the beginning of their fight to end segregation.

What makes their courage even more remarkable is how the Haydens stood up for their rights while knowing that at any moment they could be seized by law enforcement and returned to slavery.

For the rest of his life, Hayden continued running one of the most active stations on the UGRR, with as many as one fourth of the fugitives passing through Boston, staying at his home.

The author of *Uncle Tom's Cabin,* Harriett Beecher Stowe was impressed when she visited the Hayden home and met several fugitives in hiding. Her book had been written as a protest to the Fugitive Slave Law. It quickly became one of the biggest selling novels in American history, selling over a hundred thousand copies.

When people accused her of exaggerating the evil, she published a second book to prove the facts. *A Key to Uncle Tom's Cabin* included eyewitness accounts from various people including Lewis Hayden. She relied on his life story to help persuade the public of the reality of what was happening.

Hayden continued playing a major role in the abolitionist movement.

When John Brown planned his violent attempt to destroy slavery, one of the first people he consulted for advice was Lewis Hayden. Brown visited Boston several times to raise support. Each time he stayed at the Hayden home. Brown trusted Hayden to the point of having his personal mail sent to the Hayden's address.

Yet when Brown told Hayden about his plan to launch a massive slave revolt, Hayden was skeptical. There were too many flaws in Brown's plan. Hayden warned Brown his plan would fail, but Brown wouldn't listen.

When the Civil War came, Hayden's son enlisted in the Navy. That required being careful when filling out the paperwork. Joseph Hayden, who had once escaped from slavery as a child, had to make up a different birthplace on the paperwork so no one would guess his secret of being a fugitive.

Joseph faithfully served in the military for several years, reenlisting each time his term expired.

Shortly after the end of the war, Joseph died of unknown causes. The only information the Haydens received was that Joseph had been at Fort Morgan, Alabama when he passed on June 27, 1865.

The Haydens deeply grieved him yet found comfort in knowing he had died while doing what he loved.

Life moved on. Hayden became the first African American to work for the Massachusetts State Government. Later he served in the Massachusetts State Legislature in 1873.

Both Hayden and his wife lived well into their seventies. Their love lasted a lifetime.

Hayden passed away of natural causes at age 77 in 1889.

Hayden had touched so many lives that his funeral was attended by an overflow sized crowd. At the funeral, famous writer Thomas Higginson honored the memory of his friend.

"Lewis Hayden taught a well needed lesson to the whole nation. That the abolitionists were not cowards."

"All the colored soldiers loved to recall the day that Hayden sat in that room with revolvers and knives, waiting for the slaveholder to break into the house. In recognition of that service, we are glad to cast our leaf in his memory."[60]

The pastor who gave the eulogy described, *"The secret of Hayden's life was that he lived for others."*[61]

One of the most well known abolitionists of that time, Frederick Douglas, described how the passing of a *"brave and wise counselor"* had *"left a mournful void in our ranks."*

Four years later, when Hayden's wife Harriett passed away of natural causes at age 74 in 1893, she left a legacy to help others. According to the *Boston Weekly* Transcript, her will gave about $5,000 to Harvard to provide a medical scholarships for black students.[62] The newspaper marveled at how a free woman, who had been born under slavery, would be able to open the door for others to receive the education they needed.

The American dream was still alive and well no matter how hard the evil system had tried to destroy it.

3

James Oglethorpe

"A prudent person foresees danger and takes precautions.
The simpleton goes blindly on and suffers the consequences."
Proverbs 27:12 (NLT)

James Oglethorpe
1696-1785
From England

What would you do, if you were living on the frontier in the early days of America and the Native Americans came to warn you that an army was coming to destroy your community? That no one might be left alive. This actually happened to James Oglethorpe.

The story of Georgia begins in a different way than the rest of America. Georgia was founded by a strong Christian named James Oglethorpe, who had a vision of creating a place where poor families could go for a fresh start.

James Oglethorpe

Georgia was the only settlement to specifically ban slavery because Oglethorpe believed, *"Slavery is against the gospel, as well as the fundamental law of England. We refused as trustees to make a law permitting such a horrid crime."*[63]

Oglethorpe was born and raised in England where his father was a distinguished member of Parliament. When he was six years old, his father passed away, leaving his mother to raise ten children.

Oglethorpe followed in his father's footsteps, serving in the military for several years and then being elected to the same seat in Parliament as his father. His career in Parliament lasted over thirty years and sent him in a new direction.

Something happened to one of his friends that changed Oglethorpe forever. His friend, Robert Castell, was a gifted writer who published his masterpiece, only to go bankrupt in the process. When he could not pay his debts, he was thrown into debtor's prison.

Oglethorpe visited Castell in prison and was horrified by the terrible prison conditions.

Filthiness in the cells spread diseases so quickly that many people suffered and died. When Castell contracted smallpox and died in prison, Oglethorpe formed a Parliament committee to investigate the prison system.

What he found was very disturbing. Families were trapped under the crushing weight of a brutal system. Poor people who ended up in debtor's prison had no way for them to earn money to repay their debts or file bankruptcy.

Oglethorpe tried to close down the debtor's prison but was only able to get some of the prisoners released. The system itself would continue for many years with many other families suffering.[64]

Trying to find a way to give people a fresh start, Oglethorpe formed a committee to study how to create a settlement in America. This would be the place where poor people could start a new life and achieve *"The good fortune that they seek in vain at home."*[65]

In America they could own fifty acres of land, which many people would never be able to afford in England. Oglethorpe also wanted Georgia to be a safe haven where Christians being persecuted for their faith around the world could find a place of rest. He wrote to several groups of persecuted Christians in Europe, including Moravians that had been driven out of Austria for their faith. Several of these groups would accept his invitation and come to Georgia.

When Oglethorpe approached the King of England with this idea, he received approval, since it gave England more territory in the new world. Already England had colonies in Carolina, Virginia and Massachusetts. Meanwhile, Spain was colonizing Florida and might move up north to claim more territory unless there was something in the way. So the King granted Oglethorpe the land of Georgia in hopes of putting a buffer between Spanish Florida and the rest of America.

In 1732, Oglethorpe gathered about a hundred settlers and sailed to America. When they began building a community around Savannah, Georgia, one of the first things Oglethorpe did was meet with the local Native American tribes and develop a peace treaty.

To communicate with them, he hired a translator named Mary Musgrove. As the daughter of a Native American mother and British father, Mary had grown up understanding both cultures. Already she had successfully negotiated a trading post between the Native Americans and the Carolina colony.

Oglethorpe sought her help in making sure that the new colony of Georgia was at peace with its neighbors. Mary worked with both groups, making sure the needs of both were met. When the Native Americans requested help with launching a school for their children, Oglethorpe offered to provide a teacher. Soon the new school was up and running.

Yet while the colony of Georgia formed strong relationships with its neighbors, it soon found itself in trouble with the Spanish.

Spain was concerned that England was intruding on its claim to the new world.

In 1739, Spain and England tried to negotiate over their claims to America. However, the negotiations didn't work because both nations claimed all the new territory for themselves. Battles soon broke out across the new world between Spanish and British forces.

Orders were given to attack the British colonies of Georgia and Carolina before they could expand. Writing to Governor Horcasitas of the Spanish colony of Cuba, King Phillip of Spain ordered him to organize a large invasion force.

Governor Horcasitas appointed Monteano as Commander in Chief of the invasion and began preparing the ships, weapons, and soldiers.

The plan was that the Spanish fleet would sail towards Saint Simons Island on the Georgia coast. They would seize control of the island, establishing a base camp and unloading the men and weapons from the ship. Then the forces would *"Proceed northward by interior channels, devastating, laying waste, sacking and burning whatever settlements, plantations, and towns there may be as far as Port Royal. Destroy the fort and take possession of the entire country. Once Carolina is destroyed, the rest of the British colonies will follow. We already know that this area has no enemy troops to protect it."*[66]

Every effort was also made to keep these plans a secret so that the British would *"not be warned of our intentions."*[67]

Meanwhile, Oglethorpe was preparing to defend Georgia. For a long time, he had felt that they would face danger in America. With all the different groups claiming territory, conflict was inevitable. So even before setting foot on America, he had begun preparing for self-defense. Before the first group of settlers left England for America, he had them trained for self-defense by the British military.

When they got to America, he had them build strong fortifications around the settlement. They also constructed forts at strategic locations around the territory where guards could be positioned to watch for an invasion. Guards were stationed at these locations on a rotating basis.

Oglethorpe knew it still wasn't enough. If they were going to survive, they would need the help of the Native Americans.

PREPARING FOR BATTLE

Hoping to join forces, Oglethorpe took a load of gifts to the local Indian tribes. Sitting down with several tribes, Oglethorpe shared his concerns about the coming invasion. Then he listened to their concerns and promised to deal with some problems that the Native Americans had had with European traders. In return, the Native Americans promised to notify Oglethorpe immediately if they saw anything suspicious in the area. They also volunteered to train the British settlers in guerilla warfare style tactics. A mutual treaty of defense was signed with both of them agreeing to join forces in case of invasion.

That still wasn't enough. Oglethorpe wrote letters back home to ask for more help. When his letters went unanswered, he got on the first ship headed back to England. There he vigorously petitioned the King to send British soldiers to protect Georgia.

The petition was successful. Oglethorpe returned to Georgia with several hundred soldiers and their wives and children. He also brought back heavy weaponry and ammunition.

Selecting the best defensive position available, Oglethorpe stationed most of the soldiers on Saint Simons Island. Since the island was about eighteen square miles, there was plenty of land to divide up among the soldiers. Each one was given room to build a home and plant crops. Guards were stationed at strategic points around the island to watch for any approaching ships. Oglethorpe also positioned troops on the other nearby islands, including Amelia Island.

It was barely just in time. By the time Oglethorpe got all of this done, Spain was ready to launch the land invasion. Thousands of Spanish soldiers and a fleet of thirty ships sailed from Cuba to Spain's Fort Augustine on the Florida coast. Upon reaching Fort Augustine, they began final preparations for invasion.

WAR COMES TO AMERICA

Spanish scouts were sent to see how much resistance would be at the Georgia coast. They landed at Amelia Island, killed two British guards, and advanced through the island until they were discovered by the rest of the British soldiers there. Then the Spanish retreated quickly, getting away before getting caught.

When Oglethorpe heard that two guards had been murdered, he sent troops to completely sweep Amelia Island. Searching every corner of the island, they did not find any trace of the enemy. So Oglethorpe decided it was time to visit Florida and see what the Spanish were planning.

Gathering two hundred soldiers and the best Native American scouts, he advanced on the border of Florida. Catching a small Spanish fort there by surprise, he made them quickly surrender. Oglethorpe positioned a group of British soldiers there and returned home.

Oglethorpe wrote to British authorities in England and received permission to launch a full invasion of Florida. British ships from Carolina were sent to help him, while he gathered a force of two thousand soldiers and Indian warriors.

In May 1740, they sailed to Florida. Landing less than twenty miles from Fort Augustine, they captured supplies and one thousand head of cattle. Moving forward, they destroyed several Spanish forts and besieged Fort Augustine.

They were not prepared for how well the Spanish were fortified. After three weeks of vigorous assaults, Oglethorpe was forced to give up the siege and go back to Georgia, hoping he would make it in time before the Spanish returned.

Once Oglethorpe made it back to Georgia, it was time for a new strategy. Working with his Native American allies, Oglethorpe began planning guerrilla warfare strategies.

The Native Americans kidnapped several high value hostages to be used in negotiations with the Spanish. They took the nephew of the Governor and the cousin of the Commander of the Spanish invasion. The Native Americans also worked with the British to capture a Spanish ship headed for Florida with supplies and weapons.

The captured supplies came just in time. Oglethorpe was running out of everything. Knowing that far more supplies were still desperately needed, he wrote home to England, giving instructions to sell his property in England and use the funds to buy more equipment. He also begged for help from more British ships to defend the coast.

The response was pitifully small. Just a few British ships were sent to help him.

Oglethorpe worried about everything, knowing that time had run out. Now he was going to face the full wrath of the enemy. Spain was ready to launch the full invasion.

The Native Americans scouts, watching the Spanish in Florida, reported back to Oglethorpe that Spain had several thousand troops and a large fleet which looked like it was preparing to go somewhere.

Realizing he was way outnumbered, Oglethorpe frantically sent word to Carolina of the approaching danger. He begged them to send as many men and ships as possible.

Carolina wrote back that they did not care. There was nothing to worry about but if something happened then they would come.

Oglethorpe's heart sank as he read their letter. Now he would just have to rely on what few men he already had.

Eight years after Oglethorpe had first come to America, the attack finally came for which he had been preparing.

In 1742, the massive Spanish fleet of fifty-two ships and thousands of soldiers left Florida and sailed to Georgia.

The weather interrupted their journey. As they would later report to their superiors, *"A furious storm beyond any human power to resist"* rose up and scattered the fleet. Several ships were lost for days at sea before being able to find their way back to the coast.[68] The rest made it to the Georgia coast and regrouped for the landing.

Oglethorpe was waiting. Ever since the Spanish had begun strengthening their forces in Florida, the Native Americans had closely watched every move the Spanish made and reported back to him.

When the warning came that the massive fleet was on its way, Oglethorpe gathered every soldier he could find and strategically positioned them across the coastline.

To hide the fact that they were outnumbered, he had the soldiers build campfires along the coastline to make it look like they had more guards than they did.

When the Spanish ships arrived, they saw the smoke and assumed each campfire had several soldiers guarding it. So they sent one ship to see how much resistance would happen if they landed.

When the ship dropped anchor on Sea Island, they were immediately spotted. British soldiers came out of nowhere, causing the ship to pull anchor and sail back out to the safety of the harbor. The Spanish fleet regrouped and continued with their original plan to attack Saint Simon Island.

Oglethorpe and his men tried to stop them. Commandeering every ship in the harbor, he prepared them for battle. Cargo was unloaded from the ships to make room for heavy weaponry so the ships could fire back.

When the battle started, the British soldiers fired every weapon they had, keeping up a heavy bombardment of the Spanish ships as they tried to approach Saint Simon Island. For several hours they held them off. But with only a few small ships to defend the harbor, they were not able to stop the invasion.

The massive Spanish fleet fired heavy weaponry at the British until they had crippled all the British boats. None of the British soldiers were killed, but the boats were so badly damaged by the battle that Oglethorpe had to tell them to pull back. He sent them to Carolina for repairs, while he evacuated all his ground troops from Saint Simons Island and let the Spanish have it.

As Oglethorpe retreated into the Georgia coastline, he knew that as long as he was way outnumbered, his only option was guerilla warfare.

Maybe if the Spanish thought that they had won the battle they would become careless and let down their guard.

So Oglethorpe pulled all of his men back several miles where they could dig in and prepare fortifications to stand their ground. Then he asked the Native Americans to keep an eye on the Spanish as they set up a camp on Simons Island.

The Spanish quickly realized that they had a major problem on this island. There was no fresh water. Before retreating, Oglethorpe had destroyed all the wells. The Spanish quickly used up all the water they had brought with them and had to send out some men to look for more. The Indians easily captured the search party and brought them to Oglethorpe in case hostages might be needed for negotiating with the Spanish.

The Spanish sent out another search party. That one also disappeared. The Spanish were forced to ration what little water they had while sending out another search party. This one managed to find water and return safely but the water they brought back had been taken from a muddy ditch. The choice was either drinking pure filth or going thirsty. The Spanish decided to send out a much bigger scouting party to go further inland for water while also trying to see where Oglethorpe was and how much fortifications he had.

The Spanish sent over a hundred men to explore as far inland as possible. No sooner had they started on their way than their movements were reported to Oglethorpe, who took a group of soldiers to meet them.

This was a massive battle.

Fighting side by side, together the British and Native Americans attacked the Spanish, catching them by surprise.

During the battle, the Native American Chief of the Creek tribe, Tomochichi, personally shot and killed the Spanish Captain Magaleeto. While they both drew their weapons at the same time, the Native American was better skilled with guns. When Magaleeto drew his gun and shot at Tomochichi, he only struck his right arm. Tomochichi calmly pulled out a pistol with his left hand and took out Magaleeto.

When the dust cleared, many of the Spanish were dead. Sixteen were taken prisoner.

One of them escaped and warned the Spanish commander that Oglethorpe had several Native American tribes fighting with him.

Following this defeat, the Spanish Commander Monteano sent out a larger group of three hundred men. Another vicious battle took place, which ended with the British retreating. The Spanish pursued, but soon lost their trail. The Spanish continued their pursuit, coming to a place with a very narrow passage with a marsh on one side and heavy woods on the other.

By that time it had been a long day and everyone was tired and hungry. They hadn't seen any British for several miles so they figured this was a safe area to take a break. The Spanish sat down on the road to eat their lunch.

They had no idea they were being watched. Hiding in the woods, the Native Americans and British were waiting. As soon as the Spanish begin to relax, the woods came alive in what would become known as the Battle of Bloody Marsh. The British and Native Americans fired at them from every angle. The Spanish fled back to their camp, completely terrified at what had happened.

Meanwhile a British soldier had just escaped from being held prisoner by the Spanish. He told Oglethorpe that the Spanish camp was deeply divided to the point that the troops from Florida were camping separately from the troops from Cuba. Fear had spread through the camp. They were terrified of the Native Americans. After the Battle of Bloody Marsh, the Spanish had become so worried about ambushes that they would not allow any soldiers to leave their camp *"For fear of being surprised by the Indians."*[69]

Oglethorpe was thrilled at the news. Deciding to make a bold move, he took several hundred men to look at the Spanish camp. Maybe they could get an idea of the camp layout and prepare an attack.

Things quickly went wrong. When Oglethorpe got within a couple miles of the Spanish camp, he was betrayed by one of his own men.

Oglethorpe had been so desperate for men that he had written to all the other British colonies even the ones as far north as New England, asking for troops. New England had actually sent a group to help him. In that group was a Frenchman who decided he had a better chance of survival by deserting to the enemy than staying with the way outnumbered and outgunned British.

As Oglethorpe and his men approached the Spanish camp, the Frenchman fired his gun to warn the Spanish. Then he took off running, making it safely to the Spanish camp before Oglethorpe's men could stop him.

Oglethorpe had no choice but to retreat and think of a new strategy.

Meanwhile the deserter tried to gain favor with the Spanish by telling them everything about Oglethorpe. That he only had several hundred soldiers spread very thin over a huge territory. That he was running low on supplies. That the Spanish could easily wipe them out if they attacked quickly.

That was all true. And that was exactly how Oglethorpe would defeat them.

Oglethorpe went back to his fort and selected one of the Spanish prisoners of war for a special mission. Writing a letter in French, Oglethorpe gave the letter to the prisoner, released him and told him to take it to the French deserter at the Spanish camp.

The letter said that the deserter would receive all the money he had been promised. He just needed to continue deceiving the Spanish with the false information that Oglethorpe only had a few hundred men. If he could also convince the Spanish to press forward into the area where the ambush was planned and extra heavy weaponry had been hidden, then the Frenchman would receive double his salary as a secret spy.

His strategy worked. The prisoner went straight to the Spanish camp where he was thoroughly searched and the letter discovered.

The Spanish commander read the letter and believed it. It made more sense to him that the Frenchman had been sent to the camp to deceive them with false information.

Plus, hadn't the Frenchman said that Oglethorpe was expecting help from Boston, Philadelphia, Virginia and Carolina?

Just when the Spanish commander was discussing the letter with his officers, a shout was heard in the camp. British ships were seen approaching from afar.

The Spanish commander decided it was time to retreat back to Florida before they were attacked by the British.

Little did he know that these approaching British ships were just the ships that Oglethorpe had sent to Carolina for repairs after being badly damaged in the battle for Saint Simons Island. When they arrived and saw the massive Spanish fleet, they realized they were way out-numbered. They decided to return to Carolina for fear of the massive Spanish fleet.

The Spanish did not know that. They had been tricked enough times by retreating British to be suspicious of any rapid withdrawal.

As the British ships turned around and left, the Spanish were sure that they were just preparing for an ambush and *"Agreed that we should retreat for fear lest Oglethorpe should attack by land while his ships did the same by sea."*

As the Spanish troops would later explain this decision to the King of Spain, seeing the approaching British ships, *"Caused us to fear not so much the vessels in sight as the vessels which might follow in greater force. That is why we withdrew."*[70]

The Spanish packed up and sailed back to Cuba. They left so fast that they left a lot of stuff behind including heavy weaponry which Oglethorpe would find and use.

The Spanish reported back home that their mission had been a success. They had fulfilled their orders to destroy everything in their path by burning down all the settlements on Saint Simon Island. They failed to mention that these were all abandoned settlements. Blaming their failure on *"bad weather,"*[71] they would never return to Georgia.

Peace came to America. While there would be battles between the French and British settlements, the biggest battle had already been won. Oglethorpe and Georgia were finally able to live in peace and safety.

To celebrate, Oglethorpe proclaimed a day of public thanksgiving because *"It was not our own strength or might that saved us but Almighty God who rescued us from a powerful enemy. Truly the Lord has done great things for us (Psalms 126:3).* "[72]

4

John Wesley

"Wisdom is better than weapons of war
but one sinner destroys much good."
Ecclesiastes 9:18 (BSB)

John Wesley
1703-1791
From England

When James Oglethorpe founded the colony of Georgia, it wasn't just about meeting the people's financial needs. Spiritual needs had to considered as well. Believing that Christianity was an important part of American life, he set aside three hundred acres in the new world for building a church and parsonage. Then he invited a young seminary graduate named John Wesley to come and pastor in Georgia.

Wesley had been highly recommended by the Reverend John Burton whom he had met while they were both studying at Oxford University in England. Burton introduced Wesley to James Oglethorpe and recommended him for the position.

Then Burton gave Wesley very important advice. *"Through your hard work and the influence of Mr. Oglethorpe, much can be accomplished."*

"The people are babies in the progress of their Christian life and need to be fed accordingly. There's many different ways of preaching. However you do it, remember the example of St. Paul who became all things to all men that he may gain some (1Corinthians 9:22)."

"Guard yourself against the mistake of clinging to your own opinion. I mention this because people tend to deceive themselves by emphasizing the traditions of men over the commandments of God."

"The test of Christian wisdom is to distinguish between what is essential and what is optional to Christianity. Between what is of Divine and what is of human authority."[3]

Wesley thanked him for the advice and boarded the ship to sail to America. It was a long journey of several weeks. On the ship, Wesley met some very interesting people known as Moravians.

John Huss (1371-1415) pioneered the Protestant Reformation in Czechoslovakia by discovering and dying for the truth that only Jesus is the Way the Truth and the Life (John 14:6). For many years after his death, his followers the Moravians had also been persecuted for their faith. They had fought to survive for over two hundred years, having to practice their faith as a type of underground church. For years they continued practicing their faith despite heavy persecution. Oglethorpe had heard of their courage and invited them to move to the colony of Georgia to have religious freedom. They accepted the offer, boarding the ship to sail to America.

During that long voyage, John Wesley attended many of their on-board services. The more he got to know them, the more impressed he was by their simple faith in the grace of God and being led by the Holy Spirit.

When the ship encountered severe storms and became damaged, everyone else panicked. Only the Moravians remained calm. They sat and sang hymns while waves battered the ship and the sailors frantically tried to fix it.

Wesley asked them how they could be so calm. They replied that they were not afraid to die. When Wesley wrote this in his diary, he admitted being afraid of dying.

WESLEY IN AMERICA

After weeks at sea, Wesley and the Moravians arrived in America.

The harsh reality of frontier life was a brutal shock. The weather was so much colder than he had ever known. Not packing enough warm clothes left Wesley shivering upon arrival. He missed the comforts of home. Yet giving up and going home was not an option. Knowing that God had called him to serve this new community, Wesley was determined to stay, no matter how uncomfortable he was.

On Sunday mornings Wesley conducted church services, led worship, ministered communion and preached the Bible. The rest of the week he held Bible studies and prayer meetings. These meetings were well attended. Many of the settlers were Christians seeking to grow in their faith. Yet Wesley would run into trouble when he forgot the advice of his friend Rev. Burton.

Wesley was harsh to his congregation. Making up his own set of rules, he insisted on holding services at 5:00AM, 11:00AM and 3:00PM. Anyone who missed the 5:00AM service was denied communion at the other services. When people complained about the inconvenient service times, Wesley replied that this was an unbreakable tradition. He ignored how the people were exhausted from working long hours and needed evening and weekend services. Refusing to listen to their needs, Wesley berated the people from the pulpit.

Church attendance declined as people became frustrated with him. They knew the Bible better than he did. They knew what Scripture actually required and wondered why he insisted on trying to please God through sacrifice instead of faith and obedience to God's actual laws.

Finally, one man took Wesley aside and told him, *"No one ever listens to you anymore because all you ever preach is personal attacks on specific people. The people in town talk about how they don't even know what type of religion you have, because they're Protestants yet have never heard this before. And then in your personal life, you keep starting quarrels in the town. Now no one in the town will mind a word you say or want to come to hear you."[74]*

Wesley refused to listen. Thinking he knew more than anyone, he continued down the pathway of following man's opinions instead of actual Scripture. The last straw came when he humiliated the niece of one of the colony's trustees.

First, he fell in love and tried to marry her. Then he broke her heart. While she loved him deeply, Wesley had no idea how to be romantic. He would not listen to her. Most of the time they spent together, he made it clear it was his way or the highway. No matter how hard she tried to make the relationship work, he kept sabotaging it.

When he finally broke up with her, she started seeing a different man and was soon married.

Wesley was upset at her. When she brought her new husband to church, Wesley refused to serve them communion.

This public humiliation infuriated her. She filed a lawsuit, demanding that Wesley prove to the court why he refused her communion.

Wesley's pride was hurt. Instead of showing up to court, he packed up and left for England.

During the several weeks it took to sail across the ocean, Wesley had a lot of time to think.

God had a lot of time to deal with his pride.

Thinking about his 21 months in America he realized, *"The whole time I was in Georgia, I was fighting but not winning because I had failed to appreciate God's loving-kindness. I had gone to America to save others only to realize that I myself needed to be saved."[75]*

WESLEY IN ENGLAND

By the time that Wesley got back to England, he had begun to soften. He decided to let go of his pride and focus on following in the footsteps of Jesus.

This was a completely different way of life for him. Wesley had been so strict with himself for years that he had done everything from fasting until his health suffered to trying to pray for hours without rest.

He had no idea how to be led by the Holy Spirit. Maybe he could find a group of Moravians in England and learn from them how to do it.

The Moravians warmly welcomed him. For months he sat in their congregation and listened. But when they found out that he was still trying to please God with sacrifices instead of obedience, one of the leaders, Peter Bohler, told him, *"My brother, that philosophy of yours must be purged away."*

Bohler took Wesley aside and taught him simple faith in Jesus.

By this time Wesley felt like such a failure that he never wanted to go back to the ministry.

Bohler reminded him that every Christian needed to share their faith.

Wesley said he did not know what to preach.

Bohler replied, *"Preach faith until you have it. Then because you have it, preach faith."*[76]

Bohler sent Wesley to the local prison to minister to an inmate on death row. This time, instead of teaching his opinions, Wesley shared the simple Gospel of salvation through faith in Jesus and repentance from sin.

When the inmate accepted Jesus into his heart, Wesley realized it was the first real success he had ever had in ministry.

Little did he know that God had big plans for him. For the rest of his life, he would travel, preach the Gospel, and pioneer the Methodist movement which would spread across England and around the world.

Wesley would experience remarkable success in pioneering this movement because he did something that rarely happened in those days. He allowed women to speak and minister. They did much of the work for him. In a time when it was unthinkable to allow women to preach from the pulpit, Wesley personally ordained several women into the ministry. Then he sent circuit riding female pastors who traveled many miles and preached the Gospel on the neglected frontiers.

While these women were turning the world upside down, Wesley was teaching from the Bible the right of women to minister.

In a 1786 sermon, *Visiting the Sick,* he preached, *"While it has long been said 'Women are only to be seen and not heard,' that is the deepest unkindness and horrid cruelty. I don't know how any woman of sense and spirit can submit to it. Let all of you assert the right which God has given you. Yield not to that vile bondage any longer."*

"It is the right and duty of women to have a part in this ministry. You as well as men are rational creatures. You like them were made in the image of God and are called of God 'To do good unto all men (Galatians 6:10).'"

"Be not disobedient to the heavenly calling (Acts 26:19).'"

"Whenever you have opportunity do all the good you can and everyone of you 'shall receive your own reward according to your own labor (1Corinthians 3:8).'"

"It is well known that in the early church there were Deaconesses working in the church such as Phebe in Romans 16:1."[77]

GEORGE WHITEFIELD'S INFLUENCE ON AMERICA

Meanwhile, the colony of Georgia had a new pastor. Before John Wesley left, he had written to a friend in England and invited him to take over the pastorate of Georgia.

That friend was George Whitefield. They had met while they were both students at Oxford University in England. They had become well known for their campus Bible study, the *Holy Club,* which focused on pursuing God.

After graduation, George Whitefield had been ordained as a minister and invited to speak at churches in England. The Holy Spirit had moved through his ministry, touching many lives. He was also known as one of the best public speakers of that time with the ability to inspire an audience with his fiery sermons.

When John Wesley gave up on his pastorate in Georgia, he recommended Whitefield as his replacement. Whitefield accepted the invitation and sailed to America in 1738.

Upon arrival in America, Whitefield was invited to speak at several different towns. He was warmly welcomed by the various congregations and quickly became very popular in the colony.

Having much better people skills than Wesley, Whitefield easily made friends. Already he was one of the most popular preachers in both England and America. Many people were impressed by him including Lord Chesterfield who described him as *"The greatest preacher I have ever heard."*[78]

Other towns and colonies invited Whitefield to come and minister to them. When he traveled to Philadelphia and preached, this meeting was described in the *Pennsylvania Gazette.*

"Last Thursday the Rev. Whitefield preached from the courthouse gallery at 6:00PM while nearly six thousand people stood in awful silence to hear him."

"This continued every night till Sunday. He plans to preach the Gospel in every province in America."[79]

The writer of that article and editor of the Pennsylvania Gazette was one of Philadelphia's most prominent residents, Benjamin Franklin. At first, he was very skeptical of what people said about Whitefield. How could a preacher attract such a large crowd? Surely the reports must be exaggerated.

Franklin went to see for himself and realized, *"Multitudes of all denominations that attended his sermons were enormous. At first, he was permitted to preach in some churches, but the clergy began to dislike him and soon refused him their pulpits, forcing him to preach in the fields."*

"It was wonderful to see the change soon made in the manners of our people. From being thoughtless or indifferent about religion, it seemed as if all the world were growing religious so that one could not walk through the town at night without hearing psalms sung in different families of every street."[80]

Whitefield became so famous that Franklin wrote many news articles about him in his newspaper. He even devoted the front page to Whitefield several times. This was news since Whitefield was drawing massive crowds in a time when the combined population of Boston, New York and Philadelphia was somewhere between thirty and forty thousand people.

The revival quickly swept through the colonies and become known in history as the Great Awakening.

The revival had a profound effect on America. In a time when most churches rented pews and seating was segregated according to social class, this revival broke down barriers between social classes. Rich and poor, blacks and whites sat together, worshipped together, wept at the altar and received the Holy Spirit together.

Whitefield loved to preach about how Christians needed to put aside their denominational differences and work together. This was a very important message in the years leading up to the Revolutionary War when Americans from all backgrounds would have to come together to survive.

Many years later, after the war had been won and peace had come to America, Founding Father John Adams reminisced about this in a letter to Thomas Jefferson, dated December 25, 1813. *"I know of no other philosopher or theologian more profound than Whitefield."*

Adams described a sermon where Whitefield had talked about how there were no denominations in Heaven. Whitefield pretended that he walked through Heaven's Pearly Gates and asked a question:

"Father Abraham, who do you have in Heaven? Any Catholics?"

"No".

"Protestants?"

"No."

"Presbyterians?"

"No."

"Quakers?"

"No."

"Are you by yourself up there?"

"No."

"Then who's with you?"

"Just those who believe in Christ and have overcome by the blood of the Lamb and the Word of His testimony (Revelations 12:10-11)."

In that letter, Adams pointed out that the true simplicity of our faith was *"He who fears God and works righteousness is accepted by God. (Acts 10:35)"*[81]

Whitefield continued preaching across America for months. When he finally returned to his own pulpit in Georgia, the congregation had missed him. He stayed there for a time, then returned to England to receive his official ordination from the Church of England.

By this time his popularity had grown so much that many other pastors were jealous of him. As he traveled across England ministering the gospel, Whitefield found churches closed to him.

Once again he went out into the open fields and preached to whoever would listen. Large crowds attended his open air meetings.

Many were converted. Since he didn't have time to handle all the new converts, Whitefield asked John Wesley to come and organize new churches so that the new converts could grow in their faith.

Wesley discipled the new converts and many new Christian groups were launched. However, as Wesley was working with these young believers, he saw something disturbing. Many of them were doubting their salvation. They were confused by what Whitefield had preached. Wesley kept hearing people driven to desperation over fear of whether they were on Whitefield's salvation list.

For years, Whitefield had preached the doctrine of predestination: only a certain number of elect people have been chosen for salvation by God. No one else could be saved. This had caused many people who heard Whitefield's sermons to doubt their salvation and weep at the altar, tormented by fear of losing their salvation.

To calm them down, John Wesley preached the sermon *Free Grace* so that everyone would know God's free grace is available to anyone who would accept it and repent from sin. He taught from Romans 8:32 how Christ had died to save all. Thus, anyone could be saved, if they turned away from sin and accepted the atonement of Christ.

Then Wesley published a copy of *Free Grace,* distributing it far and wide to reach as many people as possible. Copies went around the world. Thousands of miles away, one of those copies reached Whitefield who had returned back to America.

When Whitefield read *Free Grace,* he found it very disturbing. He wrote a letter to Wesley, trying to correct his theology. Pleading with his friend, Whitefield said, *"I love you and would lay down my life for your sake, but I must oppose your errors."*

Then Whitefield proceeded to lecture Wesley on how *"salvation does not depend on free will. Don't make me preach against you. I'd rather die."*

When Wesley received the letter, he was not surprised. He knew exactly how Whitefield felt but he decided to take the high road.

Refusing to argue about doctrine with him, Wesley wrote back in kindness and humility.

"Thank you for your letter. Some people believe in predestination and some don't. God is speaking to both sides, but they won't listen unless they can hear a preacher who is of their own opinion. Thus, for a time you and I have different opinions, but when God's time comes, God will do what man cannot. He will make us both of the same opinion."[82]

Wesley closed his letter by creating the phrase *"agree to disagree,"* to close the issue.

Whitefield was deeply offended by Wesley's letter. How could Wesley not understand that Whitefield knew more about the Bible? Besides, how could he be wrong when he was the most popular preacher in America with massive crowds hanging on his every word?

Whitefield publicly rebuked Wesley's doctrine by publishing a book called *"An Answer to Wesley's Sermon on Free Grace."*

Wesley was deeply hurt by Whitefield's public rebuke. They would not speak again for years. Both of them insisted that they were right. Whitefield especially knew he was right because *"I receive my doctrine from God."*[83]

There were many people who disagreed with Whitefield. Even his own congregation rejected his theology.

One of the trustees of Georgia, William Stephens complained about Whitefield. *"The main drift of his sermons, morning and afternoon was the terrible doctrine of predestination which shocked all who hoped for salvation through repentance and faith in Christ."*[84]

Whitefield refused to listen to his own congregation or accept any correction at all. How could they tell him what to do?

When the congregation complained about his sermons, he would just spend more time on the road, preaching to people who wanted to hear him. That soon got him in trouble in Carolina.

Church leadership in Carolina summoned Whitefield to appear and answer for his strange doctrines and unconventional methods.

Whitefield appeared in court and defended himself.

Accused of neglecting his own congregation, Whitefield's defense was saying his only intention was to preach the gospel of Christ and that no church authority had jurisdiction over him.

The court did not accept his excuse. The prosecutor pointed out how Whitefield had another motive. All his traveling and preaching had resulted in large offerings being received from many different communities. Those offerings were draining funds from the local churches. What had he done with all this money?

Whitefield replied that all this money was being raised for an orphanage.

The orphanage was real but so was Whitefield's greed. The court was right that Whitefield was only after the money. Yet the court was unable to stop Whitefield from continuing to pursue money ahead of everything else.

When Whitefield first came to Georgia, he saw how the harsh frontier life had taken the lives of many parents, leaving many children as orphans. Hoping to make a positive difference, Whitefield asked the trustees for a land grant so he could build an orphanage. He was given three hundred acres but no money for construction, buildings, or hiring workers. This had prompted Whitefield to go on a fundraising campaign, traveling across America.

When he spoke in Philadelphia, Benjamin Franklin attended the meetings. Franklin was impressed by how Whitefield could squeeze money out of anyone.

Franklin described how while sitting in the service, *"I had in my pocket a handful of copper money, three or four silver dollars and five gold pieces but had resolved that he should get nothing from me. As he preached, I began to soften and decided to give some. By the time he had finished, I emptied my pockets into the collection plate."*[85]

Franklin later regretted giving that money when he discovered how careless Whitefield was with money.

Franklin asked questions about where all this money was going.

First of all, why build the orphanage in Georgia where construction was very expensive? Everything would have to be shipped in from thousands of miles away, which would drain the finances too quickly. There were many other places where the orphanage could be built for a fraction of the cost.

At one point, Franklin actually sat down with Whitefield and pleaded with him to change his mind.

"Georgia was destitute of materials and workmen. Sending them there from Philadelphia would be a great expense. I advised him to build the orphanage in Philadelphia and bring the children to it, but he rejected my counsel."[86]

By the time Whitefield finished his tour of America, he had raised more than enough to provide for the orphanage. Construction began as soon as he returned to Georgia.

Just like Franklin had predicted, it was very expensive. Everything had to be shipped in from a great distance. Plus, Whitefield didn't even bother taking the time to find the best price for materials. He just ordered impulsively, trying to finish the project as fast as possible.

One of the leading settlers in Georgia, Thomas Jones, noted,

"He paid an extravagant price for stones without ever consulting with anyone but himself."

When people questioned him, Whitefield justified his decisions by saying that this project *"is for the Lord Christ. He will take care of paying all expenses."*[87]

The money soon ran out. Trying to finish the project, Whitefield went deep in debt. When the orphanage was finally finished, nothing was left to hire workers or purchase supplies. The orphans who moved in had to rely on the generosity of the community. Meanwhile, Whitefield went back on the road, trying to raise more funds. This time he would be more careful in his spending. Yet he would end up trying to get money the wrong way.

Whitefield traveled back to England and fell in love with a wealthy widow. They were married and she returned with him to America.

Then he broke her heart. She had married him hoping for a happy life together. Yet he spent very little time at home with her. Most of his time was on the road. He left her at home alone while he continued traveling, preaching and taking money from good people.

When he heard that Boston had experienced a major fire, he took up a collection and sent it to the city authorities. They were very grateful and distributed it among the people of Boston who needed help. Meanwhile, Whitefield also continued fundraising for the orphanage. By the time he had returned to Georgia he had enough money to get it going.

Then he made more mistakes. Whitefield paid for several indentured servants to be imported to America in exchange for them working for free for several years.

His plan failed. Most of the indentured servants escaped as soon as they arrived in America. They went north to other colonies, found paying jobs, bought houses and began new lives. Only a few indentured servants stayed at the orphanage and worked out their contracts, but it wasn't enough people to keep up with all the work that needed to be done. Soon Whitefield was even deeper in debt, trying to keep the orphanage afloat.

Once again Whitefield was confronted with the consequences of his extravagant spending. Yet instead of taking responsibility for his mistakes, Whitefield decided to take the easy way out. He opened the door to evil, destroying thousands of lives in the process, because he was too lazy to be financially responsible and too cheap to pay honest wages to his workers.

Whitefield approached the Georgia trustees and complained that paying for labor was too expensive. Whitefield asked the trustees to change their rules. Would they consider legalizing slavery in Georgia? Then he could save a lot of money by not having to pay anyone.

The trustees were offended at the request. Didn't he know that the evil of slavery was forbidden in Georgia? Already many of the other settlers had made the same evil request. The trustees declined their request and told them to leave the colony.

The Georgia trustees did not want to bring such a horrible evil to their territory.

Yet Whitefield did. When the trustees refused, he went looking for a second opinion. To appeal to higher authority, he traveled all the way back to England to petition British authorities.

This set off a huge debate in Parliament. Some members of Parliament threatened to withhold funds from Georgia unless they allowed slavery.

The Georgia trustees refused to back down. They refused to open the door to evil. They stood for what was right because they wanted a better future for America.

As Whitefield traveled back to Georgia, he complained how *"the stubbornness of the trustees is not altering my debt load, but increasing it."*[88]

Thinking only about himself, Whitefield worried that he might be put in jail if he couldn't repay his debt of over a thousand pounds.

Trying to justify his evil intentions, Whitefield figured *"the slave trade will continue whether we participate or not."*[89]

So he wrote to a friend in Carolina and asked to borrow some slaves. His friend responded by giving Whitefield a plantation in Carolina with slaves to work it. Profits from the plantation were sent to support the orphanage.

Whitfield saw nothing wrong with this horrific plan. This new revenue stream gave him enough money to cover expenses. Trying to justify his selfishness he decided, *"This confirms my opinion that Georgia can never flourish unless Negroes are employed."*[90]

Some of the other settlers agreed. They continued petitioning the trustees to change their policies. Meanwhile, some of the settlers openly violated Georgia's law by importing slaves.

The trustees tried to enforce the law by forcibly expelling anyone who violated it.

But the settlers complained to British authorities in England.

Parliament began to look into the issue. Hearings were held.

The Georgia trustees fought back by passing a resolution. *"Those who insist that this colony can never succeed without the use of slaves are actually hindering the colony by refusing to contribute their own labor to it. Therefore they would benefit this colony by leaving."*[91]

For sixteen years, the trustees fought to keep slavery out of Georgia. Withstanding tremendous pressure from every direction, they stood their ground. But they were rapidly losing ground. More and more settlers were openly defying the law by renting slaves from Carolina. Then they began buying slaves in open defiance of the law. Finally they began importing their own slaves directly from Africa. Soon slave auctions were being publicly held in Georgia.

The trustees still would not back down. They stood for freedom. When they refused to budge on the issue, the charter of the colony was revoked by England. Slavery was permitted. Then there was nothing the trustees could do about it.

Oglethorpe later wrote, *"My friends and I settled the colony of Georgia, being established as trustees by the charter. We determined not to allow slavery there because it was against the Gospel as well as the fundamental law of England."*

"But the slave merchants and their followers caused us much trouble until at last they got the British government to favor them. When we would not allow slavery to be authorized under our authority, the government took away the charter by which no law could be passed without our consent."[92]

The trustees decided that if they could not stop the evil, maybe they could regulate it. They passed several laws that tried to improve working conditions and prevent violence toward slaves.

Yet once the floodgate of evil was opened, it would not be closed until six hundred thousand soldiers had given their lives on the bloody battlefields of the Civil War to destroy the evil system.

Whitefield's ministry continued for many more years. He continued preaching to thousands more people.

His orphanage would become a success. It would become known as the longest running charity in the United States.

Whitefield died at age fifty-five from the exhaustion of constant travel and ministry.

Then George Whitefield had to answer to God for opening the door to evil. How trying to build an orphanage had gotten him off track from the call of God on his life. How he had forgotten that God cares much more about people than ministries.

While God had used him to bring the Great Awakening revival to America, in the end, Whitefield stood before God with blood on his hands from thousands of families who suffered because of his decision.

Today historians still point to Whitefield as one of the most influential people in changing the minds of the Georgia trustees.

Whitefield's influence later resulted in Georgia becoming the roadblock to stopping the Founding Fathers from abolishing slavery as America became a nation.

Years later when the Revolutionary War came and the *Declaration of Independence* was written, the first draft included a protest against how the King, *"has waged cruel war against human nature itself, violating the most sacred rights of life and liberty. Determined to keep open a market where men should be bought and sold, he has suppressed every legislative attempt to prohibit or restrain this appalling commerce."*[93]

John Adams wrote that he was *"delighted"* with that paragraph, *"though I knew (Jefferson's) his southern brethren would never allow it to pass in Congress."*[94]

When the Declaration of Independence was presented to the Continental Congress for approval, South Carolina and Georgia demanded that the antislavery paragraph be deleted. So it was changed to read that the King *"has refused to approve laws necessary for the public good."*[95]

Years later when the Constitution was being written and the Founding Fathers of America got into a heated debate about slavery, then Georgia and South Carolina again drew a line in the sand, making it very clear they would not allow an America without slavery.

As James Madison wrote to Thomas Jefferson, *"South Carolina and Georgia were inflexible on slavery. The result is seen in the Constitution."*[96]

METHODISTS FIGHT SLAVERY

For years John Wesley tried to heal the damage Whitefield had caused.

John Wesley even preached Whitefield's funeral. Despite the end of their friendship years prior, Wesley would only have good things to say about him.

Shortly thereafter, John Wesley published a book to fight the evil of slavery. In the book, he boldly told planters something unthinkable to say in that time—that they would go to hell unless they repented and freed their slaves. His book would inspire thousands of people to join the abolition fight by petitioning Parliament and boycotting the sugar trade.

His book was distributed throughout England and America, turning the Methodist denomination into an abolitionist organization.

Wesley also ordained antislavery church leaders like Francis Asbury and Bishop Coke to run the Methodist denomination. Fighting against every aspect of the evil, he wrote into the founding articles of the denomination that if any slaveholders were converted, they had one year to repent and free their slaves or leave the church.

One of the early Methodists who lived in the South, Samuel Davis, wrote, *"In the early days of Methodism, those rules were so universally obeyed that I know of only one member neglecting them. At our quarterly meetings, where hundreds were present with their slaves, I repeatedly heard our preacher condemn the practice as a vile sin against God. Hundreds of slaves were set free by the church members."*[97]

As Methodism spread across America, it also spread abolitionism. This was very disturbing to many slaveholders when they realized the Methodists were sending evangelists to minister to their people.

The Methodists were even training many slaves to be pastors who ministered in their communities.

John Thompson was a slave working in Maryland who wrote of how when the Methodists came, *"The slaveholders became alarmed at this strange phenomenon. They appointed men to patrol the country and break up these religious meetings."*

Thompson *"was very fond of singing Methodist hymns while at work."*

The overseer got upset and punished him.

Thompson decided, *"If he struck me again, I was going to kill him. I even planned how to conceal his body but God intervened."*

Thompson later wrote how as a slave he had been inspired by reading the newspaper and hearing about John Quincy Adam's battle in Congress to destroy the evil system.

He wrote, *"Little did Mr. Adams know he was opening the eyes of the blind and setting the captive free. I read it until it was so worn that I could scarcely make out the letters. I spent many Sundays alone in the woods, thinking about it. I found out there was a place the negro could walk unfettered and enjoy the right to life, liberty and the pursuit of happiness."*

A Methodist pastor and slave gave Thompson the chance to escape. When this pastor planned his own escape with two friends, he invited Thompson to come.

Thompson was afraid to come. He'd seen enough runaway slaves caught and brutally punished. He decided to wait for a better opportunity only to quickly regret that decision. His three friends successfully escaped, taking the opportunity for freedom with them.

One day as Thompson was walking home from working, he heard God warn him to leave quickly. Putting his faith in God and never looking back, he ran for freedom.

Later he found out that if he had ignored the warning and returned home, he would have been brutally punished for helping someone else escape.

"I knew it was the hand of God, working in my behalf. It was His voice warning me to escape from the danger."

Still his journey towards freedom was difficult. He had many close calls and very few people he could trust. Traveling on the Underground Railroad, he stayed at the home of an older Christian lady. He asked her to forge a pass for him similar to the ones written by planters giving their slaves permission to travel to visit family. That way if he was stopped by law enforcement, they would let him go if they saw the pass.

The lady refused, telling him to put his faith in God, not the pass. She said, *"Let go of depending on yourself. God can't work unless you trust Him to be all sufficient. God has never failed me."*[98]

Thompson took that advice. For the rest of his journey everything would work out. He was able to cross the toll bridge while the guard was too occupied in an argument to notice that Thompson hadn't paid the toll. He made it to safety, being helped by many strangers along the way.

Thompson's former master was furious to discover his absence. Other planters were also upset at how the Methodists were teaching their slaves, *"Dangerous notions of equality and liberty."*

Virginia Governor John Floyd warned the State Legislature that too many outsiders were infiltrating plantations and teaching the slaves to read so they could read the Bible. *"They begin first by making them religious. Telling the blacks that God is no respecter of persons—the black man was as good as the white—that all men were born free and equal, that they cannot serve two masters (Matthew 6:24) and the blacks have a right to their freedom."*

Virginia responded by sending law enforcement to disrupt any Methodist church meeting that allowed slaves to attend. Their plan quickly backfired.

Soon the Sheriff of Culpepper County, Virginia wrote back to the Governor that the Methodists were fighting back. *"While the duty of our patrols is to break up meetings of slaves, the Methodists are hindering us. The other day they warned the captain of the patrol that on Friday night they were going to have a meeting. If anyone showed up and tried to touch a Negro, they would protect the Negroes."*[99]

This actually resulted in the South Carolina Legislature passing a law encouraging people to disrupt Methodist meetings and forcibly disperse them. According to Reverend Gabriel Capters, *"This law was based on the fact that Methodism was part of the most deadly opposition. It continued until ministers of that denomination ceased to assail the bondage."*[100]

As the opposition grew, Francis Asbury and Thomas Coke, who had been appointed by John Wesley to lead the Methodist denomination, tried leading it in an antislavery direction. Yet it felt like they were going upstream against an overwhelming current. They found themselves facing mob violence when they tried to preach abolitionist sermons. As they continued the fight, Asbury worried that if the Methodists ever gave into the overwhelming pressure then *"I fear the Lord will depart from us."*[101]

Knowing they had to do something, together Asbury and Coke drafted an antislavery petition to make it very clear, *"the Negroes ought to have all their rights restored."*[102]

Then they traveled through Virginia, collecting signatures to present to the Virginia State Legislature.

One of the first people they visited was George Washington. He told them how much he had hoped for America to abolish slavery.

Yet he refused to sign their petition. All he would say is that when the petition was presented, he would make his feelings known to the Legislature.

That petition would be presented to the Virginia Legislature on November 8, 1785. It was totally rejected.

The legislature was so offended by it that instead of treating it like all other petitions which were *"laid upon the table"* they proposed *"throwing it under the table."*[103]

James Madison watched this happen and reported back to George Washington that the opposition to abolitionism was growing as the slaveholders were organizing to protect their lifestyle.

Eventually the Methodist denomination would split on the issue but as long as John Wesley was alive, they remained antislavery.

Wesley lived to be eighty-seven years old, finally passing away in peace at his home in England. By then his ministry had touched thousands of people across England and America. Yet there was so much more he had wanted to do.

While lying on his deathbed, Wesley thought about how God was raising up a new generation of leaders. Already he had gotten to meet a young member of Parliament who was focused on finding God's will for his life.

Wesley was very impressed by young William Wilberforce, who was facing monumental opposition as he began the long battle to destroy slavery in England.

Hoping to encourage him, on February 24, 1791, Wesley pulled out a piece of paper and wrote him a letter.

Encouraging him to never surrender Wesley wrote, *"Be not weary in well doing. Unless God has raised you up for this very thing, you will be worn out by the opposition of men and devils."*

"But if God be for you, who can be against you? Are all of them together stronger than God? Go on, in the name of God and in the power of His might, until even American slavery shall vanish away."[104]

Just a few days later as John Wesley walked through Heaven's Pearly Gates, the letter was delivered to William Wilberforce. That letter would greatly encourage him as he began his epic battle.

5

Owen Lovejoy

"But none of these things move me,
neither do I count my life dear unto myself,
so that I might finish my course with joy,
and the ministry, which I have received of the Lord Jesus,
to testify the gospel of the grace of God."
Acts 20:24 (KJV)

Owen Lovejoy
1811-1864
From Illinois

There was a time in American history when slavery was a forbidden topic. Newspapers refused to discuss the news for fear of offending people.

Elijah Lovejoy was the newspaper editor who dared to publish the truth. They would kill him for it. Yet his death would light a fire in America that would burn into the Civil War.

Owen Lovejoy was there the night his brother Elijah was murdered. The night his own life changed forever. The night he vowed to God that as long as he was alive, he would be at war with evil.

Little did he know that in the end, he would get revenge in the best possible way.

Owen Lovejoy

On November 9, 1802, Elijah Lovejoy was born in (present day) Maine to a family who would have a total of eight children.

On January 6, 1811, Owen Lovejoy was also born in (present day) Maine to the same family.

Their parents were Christians who taught them freedom from the Bible. Their mother Betsy later wrote to remind Owen: *"Love and fear God all the day long for the fear of God is the beginning of wisdom."*[105]

When Elijah and Owen grew up, they both felt a strong calling to the ministry.

Elijah attended college in Maine, worked as a teacher and then later prepared for the ministry at Princeton. Then he moved out to Alton, Illinois to serve in the ministry as a writer of an abolitionist newspaper. Along the way, he fell in love, married and started a family.

He also started a riot.

Elijah wrote newspaper articles about freedom and civil rights which infuriated powerful enemies. Violent mobs were sent to destroy his printing press. They broke into his place of business and destroyed his equipment.

Elijah bought new equipment.

He told his neighbors that he would not compromise with evil even if it cost him his life. *"If you give up an inch of ground, there is no stopping. My duty is to stand on the firm ground of the Constitution."*[106]

His family worried about his safety.

They sent two brothers, Owen and Joseph, to help him.

In 1836, Elijah's brother Owen Lovejoy moved out to Alton, Illinois to be with him and their other brother Joseph who was already there.

During this time, the Lane Rebels had been turning America upside down by preaching freedom and urging people to vote for abolitionist candidates.

Meanwhile, John Quincy Adams was fighting the battle for freedom in Congress. He had asked people to organize community groups and send anti-slavery petitions to Congress.

Elijah and Owen answered that call and formed the first abolitionist group in Illinois.

It cost them dearly.

On August 21, 1837, Elijah's life was threatened. When he went to town to buy supplies, he was stopped by an angry mob.

They told him to leave Illinois or they would make him leave by tarring and feathering him.

Elijah stood his ground and told them he was not going anywhere.

On August 23, 1837, an angry mob vandalized Elijah's place of business and violently destroyed his equipment.

Elijah bought a new printing press with help from friends.

The mob came back, broke in again and violently destroyed the second printing press.

Elijah had to raise more money from friends but he was able to buy a third printing press.

On September 21, 1837, the mob came back and destroyed his third printing press before it was even delivered to his office.

Elijah wrote to his family. *"My office was broken up, furniture destroyed, my life threatened and I lay down at night expecting the assassin's visit."*

"Yet none of these things move me from my purpose. By the grace of God, I cannot forsake my principles. As long as I am alive, I cannot be silent (Acts 20:24)."

"I may not live to see the success of our cause but I bless God for the chance to give the best days of my life to this cause. If I die, I am assured there is a God in Heaven who sits on a throne of righteousness."[107]

On October 26, 1837, Elijah and Owen formed the Illinois Anti-Slavery Society.

On October 27-29, 1837, Elijah and his brothers held an abolitionist convention in Alton, Illinois.

The people who came, pleaded with Elijah to move away from Alton, Illinois for safety reasons. To go somewhere else that actually did have freedom of the press and he could continue publishing his newspaper in peace.

Elijah stood his ground. He replied, *"I will not flee because there is no way to escape the mob. The battle started here and must be finished here."*

"Before God and you all, I pledge myself to continue the battle until death. I will not compromise, because I fear God more than man. If I die, I die in Alton, Illinois."[108]

Yet Elijah was not going down without a fight. He was prepared for battle.

Elijah wrote to a friend about how he had to sleep with *"a loaded musket standing at my bedside. My two brothers in their rooms have three other muskets with pistols and cartridges."*[109]

His words were very controversial. At the time, many abolitionists believed in pacifism. The abolitionist movement split down the middle over whether abolitionists had the right to self-defense.

Elijah took a gun with him everywhere he went, because he knew the danger would return.

Elijah ordered a fourth printing press to be delivered by steamboat. This time he asked the boat captain to deliver it at midnight in hopes of hiding it better.

On November 6, 1837, the fourth printing press arrived. It was safely delivered to a friend's warehouse for safe keeping in hopes no one would know about it.

Everyone already knew about it.

On November 7, 1837, the violence returned. The mob came back to attack again.

Late at night, the mob gathered outside the warehouse, determined to destroy the printing press and forever silence someone willing to stand for justice.

Inside the warehouse was Elijah, Owen and several other friends armed to the teeth and ready to defend the printing press at the cost of their lives.

When the mob started making noise outside, Elijah's friends tried to make peace. One man went out to talk to the mob. He warned them that they didn't want to hurt anyone but they were going to fight for their lives and property.

1838 Drawing showing the mob attacking the warehouse to
destroy Elijah's printing press. This drawing was published in
John F. Trow's Alton Trails.

The mob replied, *"We'll take the damn press at the cost of our lives."*[110]

Shots rang out. Bullets hit the windows as the attackers tried to drive the defenders back into retreat.

Windows were smashed as the mob prepared to assault the front door.

Inside the warehouse, Elijah's friends fired back and killed someone in the crowd.

That stopped the attack. The mob left. Then they got drunk and returned. This time the mob decided to burn down the building.

The warehouse was made of brick with a wooden roof that could easily catch fire. The mob went and grabbed a ladder to climb up and set the roof on fire.

That brought Elijah and his friends out of the warehouse. They tried to grab the ladder to stop the mob from getting to the roof.

More shots were fired.

Elijah and his friends retreated back inside the building.

As long as they were in a fortified position, they were safe. But when the bullets stopped, Elijah made a fatal mistake. He opened the door to see what they were doing with the ladder.

The moment he opened the door, they fired at him.

Bullets shredded his body.

Elijah retreated back inside, closed the door, ran up the stairs and then collapsed in pain.

Owen ran to help his brother but there was no hospital or doctor to call for help. Owen held his brother and comforted him as the life flowed out of his body.

Kneeling by Elijah's lifeless body, Owen realized there was nothing he could do for him, but there was something he could do for the nation.

In that moment, Owen made a vow to God that for the rest of his life he would be at war with evil.

Elijah's wife was pregnant with no means of support. In those days, it was very rare for women to find any type of job.

Owen took care of his brother's widow by writing a book about Elijah's life to raise money for her.

To help sell more copies, John Quincy Adams wrote the forward to the book, noting that Elijah was the *"first American martyr for freedom of the press."*

Adams also wrote about how God uses regular people to change nations. That Jesus chose regular people like fishermen to launch His ministry.

How throughout history, from the time of Christ to now, the principles of Christ had slowly changed the world away from the evil system of tyranny into kindness and treating other people the way we would want to be treated.

That Christianity over the course of three hundred years dramatically changed the Roman Empire, until it had *"prevailed over the false gods of paganism, melted the system of mythology and accomplished the annihilation of Rome's three hundred thousand gods."*

"The Caesars of Imperial Rome bowed the knee to the name of Jesus. And Constantine, the master of the world, was taught by visions in the night that the cross of Christ was the sign by which he was to conquer."

"The great victory of the Christian system of morals was over oppressive governments. Yet that victory has not yet been completed."

"Christianity teaches people that that the duty of obedience to government is founded on a covenant of mutual respect for the unalienable natural rights of man and that however this covenant might be violated by power, the rights can never be extinguished and can always by power be resumed."

"Christianity has prompted men to resist tyrannical governments."

"It is the pride and glory of America that in the first great government document, they declared these truths, from the principles of Christianity, to be self-evident."[111]

Thousands of people were deeply moved by reading that book.

Many people also sent money to support Elijah's widow.

Thousands more people vowed to fight the evil system. Many people organized prayer meetings to honor Elijah's sacrifice and pray for the nation.

At a prayer meeting in a town far away, John Brown stood up and vowed to devote his life to the battle.

Meanwhile, Owen left Illinois and moved to New York City to help the American Anti-Slavery Society.

Yet his heart was not in the big cities. His heart was on the western frontier in Illinois. So he returned to the ministry to become a pastor. He had already trained for the ministry so it was a matter of taking exams to receive formal pastoral ordination from a large denomination.

He was offered a nice salary and comfortable job as a pastor for the Episcopal Church. There was one catch. In order to receive the guaranteed salary, Lovejoy had to sign a document promising never to talk about slavery.[112]

Lovejoy refused and looked for another church to pastor. He moved to Princeton, Illinois where a local church needed him.

LOVEJOY BECOMES A PASTOR

The Hampshire Colony Congregational Church had lost their pastor to illness. They hired Owen Lovejoy to preach for $600/year.

Every week he preached the gospel.

In January 1842, Lovejoy preached a powerful sermon about the Biblical duty to work on the Underground Railroad. He quoted from Isaiah, *"Hide the fugitives, do not betray the one who tries to escape."*[13]

Then he quoted from Illinois laws which hurt the Underground Railroad.

Lovejoy thundered, *"If Illinois law requires us to break God's law, then I call on you my brethren to help me trample that law in the dust."*

"Someone will say—if you violate human laws, you must pay the penalty."

"What if we are fined? Will we be the first Christians to have our possessions taken?"

"What if we die a violent death? Thus, the Lord Jesus Christ died. Thus Peter, Paul and the other Apostles died."

"Let them heat their furnaces seven times hotter. Let them starve their lions. Let them prepare their torture instruments to make us tell where the fugitives lie concealed. Can they heat a furnace as hot as the lake of fire and brimstone?"

"Have they any undying worm to prey upon the soul forever? Who then ought we to fear? We must obey God rather than man."

"By the prostrate body of my murdered brother, while the fresh blood was oozing from his chest wound, on my knees, alone with God and the dead, I vowed never to forsake the cause that was sprinkled with his blood. The oath was written in blood. It must stand."

"Thank God I am not alone and I see there are others here determined to obey God rather than men."[114]

While pastoring there, Owen also fell in love and married a widow on January 18, 1843.

The widow had three children which Lovejoy raised as his own. The widow also owned a farm which gave Lovejoy a chance to work on the Underground Railroad.

That got him in trouble with the authorities.

In May 1843, U.S. Attorney Benjamin Fridley brought criminal charges against Lovejoy for helping fugitives escape. Successful prosecution could cost Lovejoy everything including his home and farm.

When someone asked Fridley to make sure that Lovejoy was thrown in jail, Fridley surprised them with a totally different response. *"Prison? This prosecution is more likely to send Lovejoy to Congress."[115]*

The case was thrown out of court because the judge reminded the jury that Illinois was a free state. *"Slavery cannot exist here."[116]* The judge decided that masters were at fault for bringing slaves to the state of Illinois in the first place.

Lovejoy returned to his pulpit and recruited more people to work on the Underground Railroad.

Yet he knew he had another calling. He got involved in politics, trying to rally Christians to vote for abolitionist candidates.

Meanwhile, William Lloyd Garrison hurt the abolitionist movement by convincing good people not to vote.

In 1840, at the New York Anti-Slavery Convention, Garrison split the abolitionist movement in half by telling people that voting was sinful. The abolitionist movement divided between Garrison's followers and people who still wanted to vote.

Even when Garrison's words made the work harder for Lovejoy, he never gave up.

Lovejoy continued recruiting people to fight back with ballots not bullets.

On July 4, 1840, at a meeting of the Illinois Anti-Slavery Society, Lovejoy and some friends submitted a petition to encourage people to stop voting for proslavery candidates from both the Whig and Democrat parties.

Lovejoy pushed for a new third party to promote abolitionist candidates. His work helped pioneer the new Liberty party with an abolitionist platform.

The day came when Lovejoy had the joy of hosting a Liberty party state convention in the city of Alton, Illinois where his brother had been murdered.

Lovejoy also worked in the churches to get people out to vote.

On March 26, 1842, Lovejoy helped write an open letter to all churches within the Rock Ridge Congregational Church Association.

"The church's business is to reform and renovate the world—to oppose sin in whatever shape it may appear."

"The world is in league with hell. Still held in bondage by that ancient slaveholder the devil, who binds and scourges here, and then drags them down to his own dark abode (in hell) to become its tortured inmates forever. Yet the Church looks on with frosty indifference."

"Remember that Christ purchased a church with His own blood for no other purpose than laboring to secure the salvation of the entire world."

"We urge you to vote in the fear of God. To not follow a crowd to do evil (Exodus 23:2)."

"While the laws of this state forbid your harboring fugitive slaves, God's laws are supreme and must be obeyed. Isaiah 16:3: 'Hide the outcast, betray not him that wanders.'"[117]

LOVEJOY RUNS FOR OFFICE

In 1846, Lovejoy ran for Congress as a Liberty party candidate. He wanted to go to Congress for one reason. *"I want to look those slaveholders in the face."*[118]

The slaveholders were upset about Lovejoy running for office.

Violent mobs were sent to disrupt his meetings. People threw eggs at anyone who dared to attend Lovejoy's events and try to hear him speak.

Lovejoy encouraged the people to stand strong. The more opposition they faced, the more voters came to their side. *"Every egg they throw hatches a Liberty chicken which will be full grown by election time."*[119]

Lovejoy lost the 1846 election but gained new voters for the Liberty Party. Lovejoy's campaign had convinced lots of people to get out and vote instead of sitting passively at home like Garrison demanded.

Yet it was not enough to elect people to Congress. The Liberty Party struggled and slowly died.

Then the Free Soil party was founded to elect people to Congress who would fight to keep slavery out of the western territories.

In 1848, Lovejoy ran again for Congress as a Free Soil candidate.

He lost again but he won name recognition as more and more voters heard about his freedom platform.

Then Congress passed the Compromise of 1850 and Fugitive Slave Law which angered the American people.

Lovejoy thought, *"The Democrats have returned like a dog to its vomit (Proverbs 26:11). It's high time we start organizing."*[120]

To fight back, Lovejoy pulled strings and started organizing a new political organization.

On January 21, 1852, at the Illinois Anti-Slavery Society meeting, Lovejoy presented an idea to form a new third party to elect abolitionists to Congress.

On August 15, 1852, Owen Lovejoy, Frederick Douglas and Joshua Giddings (Congressman and best friend of John Quincy Adams) had a meeting to form what would become the Republican Party.

This new party was formed to fight the 1850 Fugitive Slave Law.

Lovejoy's work was barely just in time.

On May 30, 1854, President Pierce signed the Kansas-Nebraska law, opening the entire western territory to evil. This law destroyed the 1787 Northwest Ordinance which had drawn a line in the sand, forbidding slavery from expanding into the western territories. This new law allowed territories being formed into new states to choose whether they wanted to be slave or free.

That motivated a young man named Abraham Lincoln to return to politics.

Lovejoy recruited his friend Lincoln to join his new Republican party.

On August 30, 1854, the new third party was officially named the Republican party.

Newspapers in Illinois published a notice that on Oct 5, 1854, a political meeting would be held for the people of Illinois who wanted to put the government on a Republican track.

Lovejoy and Lincoln campaigned together for the Illinois State Legislature.

At the time, Lovejoy was seen as a crazy abolitionist so many people were reluctant to vote for such a controversial candidate.

Lincoln changed that by recruiting his friends to vote for Lovejoy.

In November 1854, Illinois voters rebelled against the Kansas-Nebraska law by sending both Owen Lovejoy and Abraham Lincoln to the Illinois State Legislature.

On February 22, 1856, Lovejoy worked with his team to formally birth the Republican party.

On July 2, 1856, Lovejoy was appointed to run for Congress again as a Republican party candidate.

Lovejoy also had help from the Lane Rebels.

Theodore Weld's best friend William Allen spent months traveling across Illinois, preaching the gospel and motivating people to vote for Lovejoy.

As Lovejoy would later describe in a letter to Weld, *"I had heard of William Allen as an abolitionist whom mobs could not scare, but had not seen him until one day a tall man touched my shoulder with a giant's grip as he said. 'Mr. Lovejoy, you ought to be in Congress. You're just the man to lock horns with those bellowing slaveholding animals.'"*

"I replied, 'Nothing short of a miracle could compel my congressional district to send an abolitionist to Washington.'"

"Allen said, 'I'm going to stump your district. I'll lecture wherever I can get a church, a hall, a schoolhouse, a private home or a barn. If I can't get them, I'll preach abolition under God's open air until the thing is done.'"

Lovejoy marveled at how, *"Allen did just that. He actually abolitionized my congressional district and sent me to Washington."*[121]

By 1858, he was helping Lincoln campaign.

By 1858, the Supreme Court had issued the horrific Dred Scott decision.

On February 17, 1858, Lovejoy responded with a powerful sermon which was printed in newspapers across the nation.

Lovejoy wrote, *"The demon of slavery has come out of the tombs. It has grown bold, defiant and stupid. It demands the right to walk around the whole nation, robbing the poor of their wages, trampling on the laws, polluting the territories and making its way to the free states."*

"President Buchanan do you believe the Gospel? I know you do. Tell me then, did Jesus shed His blood for cattle or to redeem real estate?"

"This idea of owning property in man is foul wickedness against God and His anointed. God never intended for human beings to be property."[122]

Lovejoy's voice was heard. People came out in droves to re-elect him to Congress.

On June 16, 1858, Lincoln gave the House Divided speech in the Illinois State Legislature as part of his run for the Senate seat of Illinois. Lincoln quoted the words of Christ to explain to the nation why slavery had to be destroyed.

(Jesus said, "Every house divided against itself shall not stand." Matthew 12:25 KJV)

At the time, Lincoln was an unknown political candidate running for the Illinois Senate Seat against the powerful and well funded Senator Stephen Douglas.

During the fall of 1858, Lincoln challenged Douglas to a series of debates at political rallies across Illinois. Everyone was invited to hear them share their platforms. History would remember these meetings as the Lincoln/Douglas debates.

Owen Lovejoy attended the debates, sat on the platform and helped his friend Abraham Lincoln.

Douglas tried to smear Lincoln as an extreme candidate, repeatedly accusing him of being like the crazy Owen Lovejoy.

At one point, Douglas insulted Lincoln by saying, *"I will bring him to his (mother's) milk."*[123]

Lincoln jumped up in anger and started walking towards Douglas.

Lovejoy jumped to his feet, grabbed Lincoln and dragged him back to his seat. In the heat of the moment, Lovejoy protected Lincoln from making a mistake that would have been reported in newspapers and could have ended his political career.

President Abraham Lincoln

Several days later on the campaign train, Lovejoy got revenge.

Late at night, Lovejoy went to the hotel where Douglas was staying.

Lovejoy brought a crowd with him, stood right outside Douglas' hotel room window and gave a long speech on freedom. He insulted Douglas by comparing him to a bloodhound chasing a fugitive. People loved it. Lovejoy became the talk of the town. Douglas did not respond to Lovejoy but did continue debating Lincoln.

On October 15, 1858, Lovejoy had the joy of watching Lincoln debate Douglas in Alton, Illinois, the city where his brother had given his life for freedom of the press.

The Lincoln/Douglas debates were printed in newspapers across the nation and read by thousands of people.

Lincoln lost the Senate election. Yet his words won the hearts of the nation and turned the unknown candidate Lincoln into a national hero.

The 1858 election also sent Owen Lovejoy back to Congress. There he gave a voice to the voiceless.

LOVEJOY SERVES IN CONGRESS

On February 18, 1859, Lovejoy gave one of the most powerful sermons of his life on the floor of Congress.

The slaveholders had been relentlessly attacking him. They had even recruited his own brother Joseph to write articles begging Lovejoy to change his extreme views and stop attacking slavery.

Joseph Lovejoy had been there the night his brother Elijah was murdered. He had helped Owen write the biography to raise funds for Elijah's widow.

Yet Joseph allegedly took money from the wrong people to change his mind. Then he turned his back on his own family and publicly attacked Owen for fighting evil. Joseph shocked the nation by publishing an open letter defending slavery.

That hurt.

Thousands of miles away, Lovejoy felt the pain.

Lovejoy responded with a powerful speech that shook the halls of Congress.

Standing on the floor of Congress, Lovejoy looked around and asked, *"Is this (Congress) an insane asylum?"*

"*Utterly incomprehensible that anyone can believe the Bible sanctions slavery.*"

"*Go look the Son of God in the face and reproach Him for favoring negro equality because he poured out his blood for them. Go settle this matter with the God who created and the Christ who redeemed.*"

"*How dare these men make the word of God of no effect through their traditions (Mark 7:13).*"

"*Slavery cannot touch anything without defiling it. It perverted the government, muzzled the press, debauched the church, corrupted Christianity and seeks to change the glory of God into a moloch.*"

Then Lovejoy quoted from Proverbs 30:20 (BSB): "*This is the way of an adulteress: She eats and wipes her mouth and says, 'I have done nothing wrong.'*"

Lovejoy stared down the proslavery Congressmen and told them that they were acting just like the offensive boldness of an adulterous woman "*who wipes her mouth and says I have committed no sin.*"

Then Lovejoy declared he would never bend to their pressure. "*I will never degrade my manhood and stifle the sympathies of human nature.*"

Even though the 1850 law had made it illegal to work on the Underground Railroad, he would never stop helping people because "*I would not have the guilt of causing man's despair or woman's agony.*"

"*Proclaim it on the housetops. Let it echo where slave catchers will hear it. Owen Lovejoy lives at Princeton, Illinois and he aids every fugitive that comes to his door and asks it.*"

"*You invisible demon of slavery, do you think to cross my humble threshold and forbid me to give bread to the hungry and shelter to the houseless?*"

"*I DEFY YOU IN THE NAME OF MY GOD!!*"[124]

On April 5, 1860, Lovejoy gave another powerful sermon in Congress to the slaveholders.

Congress was debating the Homestead Bill to give families a chance to get land in the western territories if they would live on it and cultivate it.

The debate was supposed to be about homesteading but quickly got off topic.

People were on edge after John Brown's revolt.

Lovejoy's words almost started a huge brawl on the floor of Congress.

Lovejoy started his speech: *"For several days, Congress has been debating polygamy. Since 1856, the Republican party has been opposed to the two relics of barbarism: slavery and polygamy. I want to see them both go down. The Federal government has the power to exterminate them in the western territories."*[125]

That was all he could say before he was rudely interrupted by angry Congressmen.

Mr. Cobb raised a point of order.

Lovejoy: *"I do not yield. I am entitled to the floor. I will proceed with my hour with the gentleman's permission or without it."*[126]

As Lovejoy continued his speech, he walked right over to the seats of slaveholding congressmen. He knew how dangerous they were.

In those days, Congressmen carried guns into Congress. Lovejoy was staring at a group of Congressmen who were all heavily armed and more than ready to pull the trigger.

Roger Pryor of Virginia jumped up and walked over to protest. *"The gentleman from Illinois shall not approach this side of the House, shaking his fists in our faces."*[127]

Mr. Potter of Wisconsin counter protested by reminding everyone the Republicans had patiently listened to the Democrats complain.

As he spoke, dozens of other Congressmen jumped out of their seats and came over to surround Lovejoy as he stared at his enemies.

They pulled out guns and cocked them.

The Virginia Congressmen demanded that Lovejoy walk back to his seat.

Lovejoy stood his ground.

Staring them down, Lovejoy drove the knife deeper.

"Nobody can intimidate me."

"You shed the blood of my brother on the banks of the Mississippi twenty years ago. And what happened? Thank God I am here today, to vindicate the principles baptized in his blood."

"You may shed more blood as you have threatened to do, but the blood of the martyrs is the seed of the church. The Republican party will spring up in all these slave states and these violent men will be replaced by more sensible men."

Lovejoy was interrupted again. The room exploded into anger, shouts and threats as the slaveholding Congressmen told Lovejoy that they would kill him if he kept talking.

The Speaker of the House called for order and told everyone to take their seats.

No one moved.

The Speaker of the House called for order again and told everyone to take their seats.

Lovejoy calmly walked over, stood in front of the Speaker of the House and finished his speech.

"They think that because I swore to support the Constitution that I swore to support the practice of slaveholding. Yet slaveholding in Virginia is not under the control or guarantee of the Constitution any more than it is in Brazil or Cuba. I deny that the Constitution guaranteed it. It is not there. The Constitution recognizes human beings as persons and never as property."

"Slavery is the sum of all evils. It has the violence of robbery, the blood and cruelty of piracy, and the brutal lusts of polygamy."

"This is the doctrine of devils and Democrats and there is no place outside hell and the Democrat party where the practice of such doctrines would not be a disgrace."[128]

Lovejoy's words were printed in dozens of newspapers and read by many people.

Later Lovejoy wrote to a friend how, during his speech when the southern congressmen started pulling guns, he was ready to die. *"I had made up my mind to sell my blood at the highest possible price."*[129]

In 1860, Lincoln ran for President against three other candidates including Stephen Douglas.

Lovejoy traveled around the nation, giving speeches to rally voters for Lincoln. He encouraged everyone to change the nation by using their power to vote. His brutal honesty won the hearts of many.

Lovejoy: *"People ask me if I am for Lincoln. My reply is that the Republican Party was not formed for the benefit of any one man, not even Lincoln. It was organized for the principles of freedom."*[130]

"Let us be true to our principles and God will crown our efforts with success."[131]

Senator Lyman Trumball of Illinois later wrote that Lovejoy was the most powerful speaker on the campaign trail. *"No man in the state (Illinois) ever exerted a greater influence on the masses by his speeches than Owen Lovejoy."*[132]

Lovejoy worked hard to get Lincoln elected as President. His efforts paid off.

In 1860, Lincoln defeated Douglas for the Presidency.

In 1860, Lovejoy was reelected to Congress along with Thaddeus Stevens who had been converted by the Lane Rebels. (Stevens was a brilliant lawyer who became the driving force behind the Thirteenth, Fourteenth, and Fifteenth Constitutional Amendments that destroyed the evil system.)

When the new Congressional session started, Lovejoy and Stevens worked together to support Lincoln.

The Civil War was coming. They knew it.

Proslavery congressmen kept pushing for deals. Lincoln warned Congress not to accept any deals from slaveholders. Lovejoy followed those directions and blocked any legislation that would have compromised.

On January 23, 1861, Lovejoy gave a speech warning Congress not to compromise with evil. There had already been too many compromises which hurt the nation.

Lovejoy made the point that if one state threatens to dissolve the union unless they get what they want, other states could also do the same thing.

For example, what if Pennsylvania threatened to secede from the Union over coal? What if California seceded over getting a railroad? What if Maine left the Union over lumber and fishing interests?

If they compromised, there would be no end to the demands for more compromise.

"The whole history of these compromises teaches us that these slaveowners will leap over all barriers in their unsatiable demands."

"I will not yield one hair until we settle the question of whether we have a government or not."

"It is we the people of the United States, indivisible. Not we the people of South Carolina or New York."[133]

The peace only lasted a few months.

On April 12-14, 1861, Fort Sumter was attacked and the nation slid into Civil War.

As the nation mobilized for war, Lovejoy would still not allow any deals.

Together with other abolitionists in Congress, Lovejoy kept battling the evil system until they had crushed it.

After years and years of suffering, Lovejoy finally got revenge for the death of his brother.

In April 1862, Lovejoy introduced the bill in Congress that destroyed slavery in the District of Columbia.

That was not enough.

Later that year, Lovejoy got more revenge by getting Congress to pass another law which destroyed slavery in all the western territories, *"To the end that freedom will remain forever the fundamental law of the land."*[134]

President Lincoln signed this bill on June 19, 1862.

Then Lovejoy pushed through two more laws to protect fugitive slaves that escaped to the Union Army.

On July 12, 1862, Lovejoy went to the White House for Lincoln to sign this bill into law.

Lincoln shared his frustrations on how the southern states, which had been loyal to the union, were blocking him from freeing the slaves.

Lincoln told Lovejoy, *"Oh how I wish the border states would accept my proposition. Then you, Lovejoy, and all of us, would not have lived in vain! The labor of your life, Lovejoy would be crowned with success. You would live to see the end of slavery."*[135]

Soon after, Lincoln decided that he would not allow anything to stand in his way. *"I have come to the conclusion that it is a military necessity, for the salvation of the Union, that we must free the slaves or be ourselves subdued."*[136]

On Sept 22, 1862, Lincoln used Presidential powers to issue the Emancipation Proclamation.

Lovejoy was thrilled to see the victory. At the Republican State Convention in Illinois, he told everyone how he felt like Simeon in the Bible who had finally seen salvation come at the end of his life.[137]

On June 12, 1862, Lovejoy gave a speech at Cooper institute in NYC.

He talked about the Biblical story of a demon possessed naked man who came to Jesus for help. Jesus drove the demons out then the man was able to be clothed and in his right mind.

Lovejoy talked about how a whole generation had been led astray by propaganda. How the proslavery people *"Will never be in their right mind until the demon of slavery is driven out."*

"I know this demon gnashes with its teeth, foams at the mouth and tries to hurt the nation but in the name of God and freedom it must be driven out."

"They say that slavery was in the Union. So was satan in Heaven but when he rebelled, God cast him out."[138]

During the Civil War, Lovejoy continued serving in Congress and pushing for civil rights laws as his health slowly deteriorated.

On February 22, 1864, in the last letter Lovejoy wrote, he shared his heart with a friend. *"When slavery has been swept away, I am hoping for a revival. A revival of religion, pure and undefiled that would go around like Jesus and heal the sick, cleanse the lepers and give eyes to the blind."*[139]

Then he let his friend know that he was too sick to write anymore.

Just a few days later, Lovejoy died on March 25, 1864.

Lincoln grieved the death of *"my most generous friend."*[140]

Owen Lovejoy was quickly forgotten by history.

Yet he accomplished something that will never be forgotten.

He got revenge by pioneering the Republican party which has lasted over 150 years and is still electing abolitionist Presidents, Congressmen and Senators.

And God answered Lovejoy's prayer by sending the Azusa Street Revival.

6

John P. Hale

Jesus said, "Do not fear what you are about to suffer.
Be faithful unto death and I will give you the crown of life."
Revelations 2:10 (BSB)

John P. Hale
1806-1873
From New Hampshire

John P. Hale is a name forgotten by history. Yet he accomplished something that benefits every person who serves in the Navy.

Hale was a lawyer and a Christian who believed in the Bible. He wrote about his personal faith, *"I believe in conscience, duty, right and wrong and above all in God who is over all."*[141]

"The Kingdom of Heaven is to be built up within us."

That everyone should follow in the footsteps of Christ towards *"Higher degrees of Christian excellence."*

"We lose much of the power of Christ's teaching by not understanding that He is our example. We look upon Him as so exalted that we seem to think His virtues are to be admired rather than imitated. This is an error."

"Let us honestly ask ourselves what would Jesus have done in similar situations."[142]

John P. Hale

While he was born in a time that slavery was legal, he believed it was wrong because it violated God's laws of freedom. *"God who sent his Son on Earth to announce the first principle is deliverance to the captive and the opening of prison doors to them that are bound (Luke 4:18-19)."*[143]

Hale knew that only the *"principles of Christianity"*[144] could destroy the evil system.

He also knew he was called to serve in politics.

In 1832, Hale began his political career by serving in the New Hampshire State Legislature.

In 1834, President Andrew Jackson appointed Hale to be the U.S. Attorney for New Hampshire.

In 1843, Hale was elected to serve in Congress with abolitionists John Quincy Adams and Joshua Giddings.

Hale was one of the few friends John Quincy Adams had while serving in the House of Representatives. John P. Hale and Joshua Giddings were almost the only Congressmen willing to publicly stand with Adams against the evil system.

When Adams introduced a bill to repeal the gag rule (to allow public debate on slavery), Hale voted with Adams.

That cost him dearly.

In 1845, John P. Hale was thrown out of the Democrat party for refusing to support slavery.

He lost his seat in the House of Representatives.

Yet Hale got revenge. He got involved with the Liberty Party and later the Free Soil Party.

He traveled around his home state, trying to rally voters to consider voting for a third party.

As he traveled and spoke, he told people he knew he had *"The talent and moral courage to combat and withstand the wicked influences of corrupt, slaveowners in Congress."*[145]

1848 Political Cartoon showing all the candidates fishing for different interests. Hale is pictured in the middle.

While many other Congressmen took money from powerful political interests, Hale refused to take a dime that he did not earn as salary.

On April 12, 1845, he gave a speech explaining why he had left the most powerful political party.

Hale said there comes a time when every politician has to decide *"whether he should obey God or man."*[146]

God's will was clear. *"As long as God is on the throne of eternity. He looks upon human bondage as sin."*[147]

Hale's voice was too powerful.

The other side sent future President Franklin Pierce to debate Hale.

On June 5, 1845, the debate was held at a church in Concord, New Hampshire.

By the time the debate came, Hale had become discouraged at the heavy opposition and deep pockets that opposed him.

Yet when he arrived at the church being used for the debate and saw a massive crowd waiting to hear his voice, he was encouraged.

Hale took the stage and spoke for two hours on the evil of slavery and the duty to oppose it.

Then he sat down and listened as Pierce took the floor.

Pierce threw false accusations at him, saying he was trying to destroy the Democrat party.

When Pierce finished and sat down, Hale was given the last word.

Hale went to the pulpit and gave one short powerful statement that resonated with the audience. His words would be published in newspapers across the nation, encouraging thousands of other people to stand with him against the evil system.

Hale turned to the crowd and grieved at how the nation was suffering because *"the truth is ridiculed."*

"I knew they would label my name as evil. I knew they would accuse me of being ambitious."

"But the only ambition I have is that one day when my earthly career is finished and my bones are laid to rest beneath the New Hampshire soil, then my tombstone will say that I sacrificed political office, position and power rather than bow down and worship slavery."[48]

(Hale is referring to the Bible story in Daniel 3:16-28 of Shadrach and his friends who refused to bow down and worship the golden image when everyone else did.)

Those words got Hale re-elected to Congress.

Those words would be remembered as the "Hale storm" that turned New Hampshire upside down.

At the time, the two major political parties were the Democrats and the Whigs. Any other political party was considered too weak to win.

Hale proved them wrong.

As a third party candidate, Hale was elected to serve in the Senate from 1847 to 1853.

In a time when many politicians were motivated by the deep pockets of the proslavery side, Hale stood for justice. He stood alone in the Senate while John Quincy Adams was standing alone in the House of Representatives.

In the Senate, Hale fought every aspect of the evil system. He tried introducing bills to abolish slavery but those bills quickly died.

On June 23, 1848, Hale brought a bill to abolish slavery in the District of Columbia. His idea was that since D.C. had no state government, Congress had authority to pass legislation over it.

The opposition was overwhelming. The bill died quickly.

Hale worried about the reality that slavery would expand into the western territory. That the *"clanking of chains and cries of agony would reach the ears of God, calling for vengeance upon us if we stayed silent and did nothing to prevent so great a wrong."*[149]

Hale was right.

Hale had returned to Congress just in time to face the worst bill in the history of the nation.

The Compromise of 1850 was supposed to save the union. Yet hidden within the bill was the Fugitive Slave Law (FSL) which opened the entire western territory to the evil system. This law gave slave catchers the ability to hunt fugitives in free states and drag them back to bondage.

Hale fought this law but he was not able to stop it. It was signed into law by proslavery President Millard Fillmore.

Hale grieved this tremendous injustice. He wrote how people were saying the 1850 law had brought peace but any peace would be short lived as the nation slid into Civil War.

Hale pointed to Jeremiah 6:14 which describes people saying *"Peace, peace but there is no peace."*

Hale warned Congress: *"Everybody is pleased (at 1850 law) except a few wild fanatics."*

"Let not the gentlemen deceive themselves (James 1:22)."

"There is no peace to those who think they have successfully dug the grave for the hopes and dreams and freedom of many. No sir. That peace will be short and the rejoicing turned into mourning (James 4:9)."[150]

Hale was right again.

As soon as the law passed, slave catchers went to Boston and tried to arrest Shadrach Minkins who had escaped from slavery.

The people of Boston violently interfered.

Shadrach escaped but the people who helped him were put on trial.

Hale was asked to be their lawyer. Helping him was another lawyer named Richard Henry Dana.

At one point during the trial, Hale gave a powerful speech that inspired the nation when it was published in the newspapers.

"John Debree claims that he owns Shadrach. Owns what? Suppose Debree says that he owns the moon and has exclusive right to its light. Would the jury agree? And yet the moon and earth will crumble and decay while the soul of the poor hunted Shadrach shall live on with God."[151]

Hale won the case. Years later, it would be discovered that the lone juror who stopped the prosecution from conviction was the same man who had helped Shadrach escape on the Underground Railroad.[152]

Yet defending the Underground Railroad cost Hale his Senate seat. He lost the 1852 election and went back to practicing law.

He told his friends that he was willing to sacrifice his career to help other abolitionists be elected.

Lewis Tappan was a wealthy businessman who funded abolitionist candidates for political office.

Hale told Lewis Tappan, *"Do not hesitate to sacrifice me if necessary. Next to an election for the long term, I should enjoy a good old fashioned fight with an open field on the slavery issue."*[153]

(Hale was saying that he can still give political speeches in open fields even if he can't win an election.)

In 1854, the Kansas Nebraska law brought Hale back to Congress.

The American people were furious that Congress passed another law allowing slavery in the western territories.

When Kansas settlers voted for a free state and free local government, President Pierce threatened to use the full force of government against the Kansas settlers who hoped for a free state.

The Kansas settlers soon found themselves suffering from constant threats of violence.

The Republican party was formed to fight the evil system.

In 1855, Hale was elected to the Senate (as a Republican) just in time to fight for the rights of Kansas.

From 1855 to 1865, Hale served in Congress as the Senator from New Hampshire.

Hale gave a speech about how President Pierce was insulting the honest people of Kansas by calling them enemies just because they wanted a free state.

Hale told Congress, *"Pierce has no right to insult them. When he does, he insults the office of President. When he denies the issue, I will throw the issue right back in his face."*[154]

While many people in Congress lobbied for whoever paid them the most, Hale fought for the rights of those without money or hope.

He opposed debtor's prison.

He opposed having a powerful central bank because he worried the banker's intentions were *"hostile"* to democracy and *"Destructive to the people's interests and dangerous to freedom."*[155]

Hale also opposed the gag rule that was used to silence Adams from bringing abolitionist petitions.

Hale was a voice for people who were silenced. Hale used his seat in Congress to help working people who were often ignored by Congress.

While many Congressmen only advocated for the rich or those who could line their pockets, Hale stood for those who had no one to stand for them.

While many other abolitionists did nothing, Hale used his seat to fight for what was right.

While Hale might not have been able to accomplish everything he wanted, he accomplished something really important.

HALE MAKES HISTORY

The first time Hale was elected to Congress, he had fought for the rights of regular people by trying to abolish flogging as a form of punishment in the Navy.

Hale introduced this bill in the House of Representatives, the very first term he served in Congress. His bill passed the House but then died in the Senate.

Years later when Hale was elected to the Senate, he tried again.

In 1848, Hale pushed the Senate to pass a resolution requiring the Secretary of the Navy, John Mason, to investigate and report back to Congress on how the Navy punished its men for their mistakes.

This report was surprising.

Hale discovered that the Navy gave their men a ration of alcohol but then punished the same men for drinking the alcohol and getting drunk.

Hale found that the Captain of the U.S. Pennsylvania had ordered its men to be flogged 239 times in 1848.

"On the U.S. ship Marion in only 38 days from December 1, 1847 to January 8, 1848, 23 sailors were punished with 439 lashes for drunkenness and desertion. Thus you degrade and brutalize the sailor by law and then by law flog him for being exactly what you made him."[156]

Hale knew it was wrong to humiliate men who had volunteered to serve their country.

Hale suggested abolishing both the alcohol ration and the punishment for being drunk.

Other Congressmen disagreed.

Senator George Badger of North Carolina protested Hale's ideas saying: *"Flogging remains the best means of maintaining naval discipline. The only alternatives are confinement or death."*[157]

Hale wondered why the U.S. Navy still allowed flogging as a form of punishment for enlisted men when this type of punishment had been abolished by the U.S. Army. How could the Navy treat their own this way when even prison inmates were spared this humiliation?

Hale won the battle.

Several years before the Civil War, in 1850, Hale successfully abolished flogging as a form of punishment in the Navy.

Hale also remembered the people who had been forgotten: the men working on merchant ships who often suffered the same punishment.

As a skilled lawyer, Hale wrote the law to also abolish flogging in the private sector on merchant ships.

Text of Hale's law: *"Flogging in the Navy and on board vessels of commerce, be hereby abolished from the passage of this Act."*[158]

Hale won the battle by including this one tiny sentence inside a spending bill that the military needed for sufficient funding.

The law was passed on Sept 18, 1850.

After his bill passed, Hale was very popular among the military.

He received letters from Navy men who were very grateful someone had fought for their rights.

Hale was invited to visit the U.S.S. Germantown. During his tour, *"The crew manned the rigging and gave three cheers for him."*[159] They also had a special present for him.

The sailors of the U.S.S Germantown had pooled their money and created a commemorative medal to honor Hale.

When the Civil War came, Hale continued serving in Congress.

When the South left the Union, many southern Congressmen left Congress.

That shifted the balance of power. That destroyed the proslavery majority that had ruthlessly ruled Congress for decades.

Once the proslavery majority had left Congress, the abolitionists in Congress started passing all kinds of civil rights bills.

Hale voted for all of them.

In 1862, Hale had helped pass a bill to protect and free slaves who had escaped to the Union Army. The legal theory was that by freeing them, then they could not be used to assist rebels against the government.

Hale said, *"The Constitution was made for a time of peace and civilized society, not the emergencies of an armed rebellion."*

"These rebels have their hands red with the blood of our brethren. The time has come that Congress should show these rebels that the Constitution and laws were not made to protect disloyal people who would subvert the Constitution and destroy the country."[160]

The American people kept fighting the evil system until it was destroyed.

After the war, Hale was thrilled to see the end of slavery.

When the Thirteenth Amendment to the Constitution came, Hale gave a speech on how: *"This is a day that I and many others have long fought for. The great sin of slavery is swept away without apology, and we can stand in this time as soldiers of old Christianity and the new civilization, going to battle with every purpose of our hearts in agreement with God in Heaven."*[161]

After the war, Hale was given a new assignment.

President Lincoln appointed him to serve as the U.S. Ambassador to Spain.

On April 14, 1865, Hale met with Lincoln at the White House.

Lincoln gave him instructions for diplomatic service and asked Hale to keep the State Dept informed of everything that happened.

That night Hale sailed to Europe on a ship.

That night Lincoln attended a play at Ford's theatre.

John Wilkes Booth was in love with Hale's daughter Lucy and had asked her to marry him.

When Booth died, on his body was found a picture of Hale's daughter Lucy that he had treasured.

John P. Hale served as Ambassador to Spain for four years. Then he returned home and retired to enjoy his last few years with his family.

Hale passed on November 18, 1873.

At his funeral, the pastor preached on Jesus' words in Revelations 2:10: *"Be faithful unto death and I will give you the crown of life."*

Hale's dream came true.

Not only did he live long enough to see the end of slavery, he was buried with his powerful words enshrined in stone: *"He who lies beneath, surrendered office, place and power rather than bow down and worship slavery."*[162]

Those words were also written on something else.

The State of New Hampshire honored Hale's legacy by building a statue of him at the State Capitol. The Statute also bears in stone Hale's powerful words that he would never bend to the pressure of the evil system.

7

John Brown

Jesus said, "Blessed are you when people insult you, persecute you, and
falsely say all kinds of evil against you because of Me.
Rejoice and be glad, because great is your reward in heaven."
Matthew 5:11-12 (BSB)

John Brown
1800-1859
From Torrington, Connecticut

The Civil War started in Kansas. Abolitionists were getting viciously attacked. It had gotten to the point where they constantly had to be prepared to defend themselves. Some were getting murdered in cold blood.

John Brown worried about his sons who lived there. With all the violence happening in Kansas, what would happen to them?

The story of John Brown begins long before the ill-fated raid on Harper's Ferry. It begins way out on the western frontier where he raised a family while fighting for social justice.

John Brown Photo Taken in 1850 by Levin Corbin Handy

Brown was a farmer, trying to carve a living in the Pennsylvania wilderness. He had two marriages that produced a total of twenty children.

His first wife passed away from what might have been childbirth complications because she died after giving birth to their seventh child.

Brown soon remarried. His second wife gave birth to thirteen children. All of his twenty children were needed to work the farm.

Life on the frontier was so difficult that some of his children died at a young age. The ones that survived, worked night and day to help the family on the farm. Brown also tried and failed at various businesses. When things didn't work out, he moved to Ohio and tried again. His businesses failed again. Soon he would have to file bankruptcy and start over.

While Brown failed over and over at business, the one thing he succeeded at was being an abolitionist.

Brown was twelve years old when the War of 1812 happened. During that time, he was raising cattle on his father's farm. When the time came to drive the cattle to market, his father sent him and the cattle to Pittsburg, Pennsylvania. While in the city he stayed at a hotel and made friends with a teenage black slave who was living at the hotel.

The black teen was treated very badly. When Brown tried to protect him, he was told to mind his own business. Brown hated how he felt helpless to help his friend but realized he had to find a different way to fight the evil system.

When Brown grew up and had his own farm, it was always open to escaping slaves on their way to Canada.

When he moved to Ohio, his farm was close enough to Canada to be the perfect hiding place for many people. For years his family operated a very successful Underground Railroad (UGRR) station. They built a secret hiding place underneath the barn. It vented to the outside for fresh air but was so well hidden that even if you stood on top of it, you would not notice it. Brown also provided transportation to escaping slaves, sometimes taking them in a horse drawn wagon long distances to the next hiding place.

That was not enough. Brown believed in something so radical, most people thought he was crazy.

He believed that everyone was born equal. That the church should treat everyone equally. Soon that got him into trouble.

Brown was a strong Christian who read his Bible daily and took his family to the local church in town.

In 1837, his church joined with a few other churches to hold a revival service. Everyone was invited. What happened next was later described by his son, John Brown Jr.

"Invitations were sent out to church folks in adjoining towns and soon the church was crowded. There were at that time in Franklin a number of free colored persons and some fugitive slaves. These became interested and came to the meetings, but were given seats by themselves, where the stove had stood, near the door—not a good place for seeing ministers or singers."

"Father noticed this. At the beginning of next evening's meeting, he rose and called attention to the seating arrangement. He said that God was not a respecter of persons (Acts 10:34). He then invited the colored people to occupy his pew. The blacks accepted, and all of our family took their vacated seats."

The Holy Spirit moved that night. Hearts were touched. The pastor, sitting on the platform, stood up and gave up his seat to another. For the rest of the meetings, *"The blacks continued to occupy our pew and our family the seats around the stove."*

Some of the ministers got upset. They visited John Brown and tried to change his mind. But Brown gave them a lesson on the Bible they would never forget.

Sometime later the Brown family received a letter asking them to leave their Congregational church. *"Father, on reading the letter, became white with anger. This was my first taste of the proslavery diabolism that had entrenched itself in the church."*[163]

That got them in trouble with the town. The Brown family soon found themselves ostracized from polite society. After that Brown never went back to a church. His wife and children would attend church but he refused.

Brown figured that if the church leaders wouldn't listen, he would find someone who would. So through the years, he visited nearby public schools and talked to the children about social justice.

Years later one of those children, Henry Carrington, would describe how Brown came and talked to the students around the same time Brown was thrown out of church. This student grew up in Torrington, Connecticut, the same town where Brown had been born.

Carrington wrote, *"When I was a boy and went to school there came into the school room one day a tall man with grey hair, who said to the boys something about Africa, the evil of the slave trade, and the wrongs and sufferings of the slaves. Then said, 'How many of you boys will agree to use your influence whatever it may be, against this great curse, when you grow up?'"*

"Another boy and I stood up. Then this man put his hands on their heads and said, 'Now may my father in Heaven, and Christ, and the Holy Spirit, which gives strength and comfort, enable you to keep this promise.'" [164]

While Brown left the church, he did not leave the Lord. He was often seen reading his Bible, which had taught him about freedom. In his own words he described his faith. *"I have always been delighted with the doctrine that all men are created equal. To my mind it is like the Savior's command, 'Thou shalt love thy neighbor as thyself,' for how can we do that unless our neighbor is equal to yourself?"* [165]

As the years passed, he continued to talk about his walk with God. *"I am not a stranger to the way of salvation by Christ. From my youth I have studied much on that subject, and at one time hoped to be a minister myself, but God had another work for me to do. To me it is given, in behalf of Christ not only to believe on him, but also to suffer for his sake (Philippians 1:29)"* [166]

When he had to travel for business, his letters to his family often described his love for God. In a letter to his family dated June 23, 1859, he wrote, *"Dear wife and children, my best wish for you all is that you may truly love God and His commandments."* [167]

Then at the end of his life, he left a will providing money to buy the best available Bibles for each of his sons and daughters. Brown wanted them to spend $5 per Bible in a time when a day's wage was $1.50.

As the years passed, Brown again moved his family, hoping for a fresh start. They lived for a time in Springfield, Massachusetts. Again Brown connected with other abolitionists to operate the UGRR. Again he helped fugitives escape. Again his business ventures failed. So he moved his family to North Elba, New York.

One day the famous explorer, Richard Henry Dana, was traveling through New York. He got lost in the woods and ended up hungry with nothing to eat. He stumbled across Brown's farm and knocked on the door, hoping for scraps. They invited him in for a meal.

When Dana sat down at the dinner table, he saw something unusual for that time. *"Brown and their large family of children with the hired men and women, including three negroes, all sat at the table together. Their meal was neat, substantial and wholesome. The family showed so much kindness."*[168]

Life moved on while the world turned upside down.

KANSAS-NEBRASKA LAW

In the early days of America, when it was thirteen states and a big western frontier, in 1787, the Founding Fathers passed the Northwest Ordinance, forbidding slavery from the western territory.

In 1820, Congress passed the Missouri Compromise, overturning the Northwest Ordinance and opening the whole western frontier to slavery. The people pushing the evil system would not rest until they gained the whole new territory.

Then in 1854, when Kansas and Nebraska wanted to form state governments, Congress had to decide again if slavery would be allowed in the west.

At the time, America consisted of 31 states, split almost evenly between slave and free. For years the proslavery forces had controlled the federal government by controlling the seats in Congress and who was appointed to the Supreme Court. The slave states wanted a majority in Congress so they could ram through as many proslavery laws as possible. Now that there was a huge western territory opening to settlement, they hoped they could create more proslavery states out of the western territory, giving them more seats in Congress.

In 1854, Senator Stephen Douglas proposed the Kansas-Nebraska bill. People wondered why, he claimed to know what was best for Kansas, when he was actually representing the state of Illinois. Douglas said that his bill would allow the Kansas people to choose for themselves whether it would be a slave or free state.

When the Kansas-Nebraska bill was passed by Congress, it ignited a violent war for territory.

Abolitionist families began moving to Kansas, hoping to keep it a free state. In 1854, they settled on the Kansas River, forming the town of Lawrence. As soon as they arrived, they were threatened with violence.

Kansas was located right next to the slave state of Missouri. It was easy for proslavery forces to hire thugs in Missouri and send them to disrupt abolitionist settlements in Kansas. When the town of Lawrence had not even been built yet and the families were still living in tents, they were visited by an angry mob.[169]

Late one night, over 200 rough looking men showed up at Lawrence, Kansas. They told the abolitionists to leave or things would get bad for them. Nothing happened that night, but a war was started.

More and more settlers moved to Kansas. By November 1854, the first election was held for representation in Congress. Proslavery forces publicly called for interference.

One of their leaders, John Stringfellow, made his feelings clear, saying, *"Mark every scoundrel who is the least tainted with abolitionism or free soilism and exterminate him. Enter every election district in Kansas and vote at the point of the bowie knife and revolver. Never submit. There is no appeal from the will of the slaveholding interest."*[170]

No one was surprised when Stringfellow was elected to the Kansas legislature.

Missouri Senator and slaveowner David Atchison publicly told *"Every county in Missouri"* to *"do its duty to send 500 young men"* to settle questions *"peacefully at the ballot box."*[171]

His voice was heard. On election day of November 1854, the border ruffians came over from Missouri and voted in the election. Three thousand votes were counted in an election when there were only fifteen hundred legal voters in the territory.[172] The proslavery candidate Mr. Whitfield won and was sent to Congress.

Kansas held another election in March of 1855. Again the border ruffians voted in the election, putting a proslavery majority in the Kansas legislature.

Brown's son John Jr. described what happened in a letter.

"An election for a first territorial legislature had been held on March 30, 1855. On that day, residents of Missouri on the border came into Kansas by the thousands and took forcible possession of the polls."

"The evening before and the morning of election, nearly 1,000 Missourians arrived, well armed, at Lawrence in wagons and on horseback with rifles, pistols, bowie knives and two pieces of cannon loaded with musket balls."

"Although but 831 legal electors in the territory voted, there were no less than 6,320 votes polled. They elected all the members of the legislature with a single exception in both houses, two free soilers being chosen from a remote district which the Missourians overlooked or didn't care to reach."[173]

The newly elected politicians wasted no time. Taking control over Kansas, they quickly wrote the Lecompton State Constitution with oppressive laws.

They made it illegal to distribute abolitionist pamphlets. Even talking about emancipation became a crime punishable by five years in prison. Then they started the process of asking Congress to admit Kansas as a slave state.

The people of Kansas were furious. They hadn't moved to Kansas to have their voice ignored and their vote cancelled. They formed their own legally elected legislature.

On October 23, 1855, they met together and wrote the Topeka State Constitution, forbidding slavery in Kansas.

That scared the proslavery forces in Congress. Just a few weeks later, when Congress reconvened, President Franklin Pierce slammed abolitionist settlers for disrupting their plans for Kansas. Disregarding the will of the voters, he appointed a proslavery governor.

The battle was just beginning.

The proslavery side was willing to do anything to win. Border ruffians continued threatening innocent people. Then they carried out their threats and the real violence began.

On October 25, 1855, Samuel Collins was murdered for wanting a free Kansas. The killers went unpunished.[174]

On November 22, 1855, William Dow was murdered for wanting a free Kansas. His body was left to rot in the road to threaten other settlers.

While the community begged law enforcement to do something, the murderer was never charged. From that point on, it was open season on abolitionists in Kansas.

On December 6, 1855, Thomas Barber came home to find border ruffians waiting for him. They demanded he leave with them. He refused. They killed him in broad daylight for wanting a free Kansas.

As the violence escalated, Kansas settlers wrote to Congress begging for help. If their own state leaders would not listen to them, maybe the abolitionists in Congress like Senator Charles Sumner would. He did.

Then he made the whole nation hear their voice.

On May 19, 1856, as Congress was debating whether to admit Kansas as a slave state, Sumner gave a speech in Congress that shocked the nation.

He read letters from the Kansas settlers describing the violence they faced:

"Our citizens have been shot at, and in two instances murdered, our homes invaded, hay ricks burnt, corn and other provisions plundered, cattle driven off, all communication cut off between us and the States. Wagons on the way to us with supplies were stopped and plundered. The drivers were taken prisoners, and we are constantly expecting more attacks."

"Nearly every man has been armed in the village. Fortifications have been built up, by nonstop labor, night and day. The sound of the drum and the tramp of armed men resounded through our streets, families fleeing with their household goods for safety. Day before yesterday the report of cannon was heard at our house, from the direction of Lecompton."

"Last Thursday, one of our neighbors — one of the most peaceable and excellent of men — on his way home, was attacked by a gang of twelve men on horseback, and shot down."

"Over eight hundred men are gathered under arms at Lawrence. As yet, no act of violence has been perpetrated by those on our side. No blood of retaliation stains our hands. We stand ready to act purely in the defense of our home and lives."[175]

That speech would get Sumner brutally punished. The slave system would not tolerate any opposition. They sent Congressman Preston Brooks to show him who was boss.

Late one night while Sumner was finishing up paperwork, sitting at his desk on the floor of the Senate, Brooks physically assaulted him. Sumner was brutally beaten. The beating was so severe that he would be disabled for over a year. Months would pass before Sumner could get out of bed, let alone return to the floor of Congress.

When news spread of the attack, the nation split down the middle over it. Most people were furious that a U.S. Senator could be beaten on the floor of Congress for suggesting that slavery was evil.

The proslavery side was thrilled that the pesky abolitionists had been taught a lesson. They also wanted the Kansas settlers to be punished for interfering with the future of Kansas.

Some of those Kansas abolitionists were John Brown's sons.

BROWN FAMILY IN KANSAS

In 1854, the same year the Kansas Nebraska bill was passed, Brown's oldest sons decided to move to Kansas for a fresh start.

At the time they were still living in Ohio. Their crops had been destroyed by a severe drought, making them look for other options to make a living. They had heard that free land was available to anyone willing to farm on it. Maybe Kansas would be a better place to raise cattle.

Brown's son John would later describe, "*During the years 1853-1854, most of the northern newspapers were not only full of glowing accounts of the extraordinary fertility, healthfulness and beauty, of the Kansas territory, the newly opened for settlement but of urgent appeals to all lovers of freedom who desired homes in a new region to go there as settlers and by their votes save Kansas from the curse of slavery.*"[176]

In those days, travel was very difficult because as John described, *"At this time there were no railroads west of St. Louis."*[177]

The four oldest sons were John Jr., Jason, Owen and Fred. The sons decided that since John and Jason had families, they would take their wives and children and travel by railroad as far as possible, then travel by river steamboat to Kansas. The two younger sons, Owen and Fred, who did not have wives or children, would travel by horseback to drive cattle all the way from Ohio to Kansas. Their eighteen year old brother Salmon also traveled with them, to help them with the cattle.

It was a rough journey that took months. They actually started in the fall of 1854, traveled by water to Illinois, then when winter snow came, had to stop in Illinois, and find shelter. The three sons driving the cattle did their best to take care of them, but still some of their best cattle were stolen.

Winter disrupted their travel, making them wait until the snow thawed and they could continue their journey in spring of 1855. The three sons driving cattle left Ohio in October 1854 and arrived in Kansas in April 1855. They were the first of the Brown family to arrive.

Meanwhile, the two sons traveling by steamboat found out they had much bigger problems. Someone on the boat was sick. The sickness soon spread throughout the steamboat. Jason's four year old son Austin died of cholera.

There was more bad news. The steamboat was carrying a large group of rough looking men. Once onboard, as Brown's sons talked to other passengers, they realized most of the other passengers were pro-slavery. That they had been paid to move to Kansas to cause trouble. These men would soon be their neighbors.

John wrote to his father, *"Every slaveholding state from Virginia to Texas is furnishing men and money to fasten slavery upon this glorious land. They boast that they can obtain possession of the polls in any of our election precincts without having to fire a gun."*[178]

When the sons traveling by steamboat arrived in Kansas in May of 1855, they liked the area.

John wrote back to their father, *"Arrived in Kansas, her lovely prairies and wooded streams seemed to us like a haven of rest. At once we set about the work. Our tents sufficed for shelter, until we could plow our land, plant corn and other crops, fruit trees and vines, cut and secure hay enough of the waving grass to supply our stock the coming winter."*[179]

Life was still dangerous on this new frontier. Within a few days of arriving in Kansas, they were visited by the locals. Several heavily armed men rode up and asked them if they were proslavery or not.

Jason replied, *"We are abolitionists."*

That was the wrong answer. Jason would later describe, *"From that moment we were marked for destruction. Before we had been in the Territory a month, we found we had to go (everywhere) armed and be prepared to defend our lives."*[180]

One of those men who threatened the Brown family was Martin White. He would later return to fulfill his threats.

Brown's sons knew they didn't have enough protection. Worried for their families, they wrote to their father, asking for weapons.

For five brothers to defend their family they only had:

"1 good rifle

1 poor rifle

1 revolver

1 small pocket pistol

1 Bowie knife

2 sling shots."

That was their only protection against what his sons described as: *"Thousands of the meanest and most desperate men, armed to the teeth with revolvers, Bowie knives, rifles and cannon, not only thoroughly organized, but paid by slaveholders."*[181]

John concluded his letter by asking his family to please send enough weapons that each man would have his own rifle, pistol and bowie knife. If there was going to be a war, they wanted to be ready.

At the time, Brown was still living in New York with his wife and the rest of his children. When he received the letter, he gathered as many supplies as possible and came to Kansas to help them.

By that time, Kansas had begun to divide itself. The proslavery settlers had formed their own towns. So did the abolitionists.

Then came the war.

George Grant was living in Kansas on Pottawatomie Creek in 1854.

He described, *"My father John Grant came from New York and settled on Pottawatomie Creek in 1854. There was a company of Georgia border ruffians camped about four miles away from us who had been committing outrages upon the free state people. Our proslavery neighbors, the Shermans, the Doyles, and Mr. Wilkinson, were in constant communication with them. They had a courier who went backward and forward carrying messages."*

"In the spring of 1856, William Sherman had taken a fancy to the daughter of one of his free state neighbors and had been refused by her. The next time he met her, he used the most vile and insulting language toward her."

"Sherman then drew his knife and said to the young woman, 'The day is soon coming when all the damned abolitionists will be driven out or hanged. We are not going to make any half way work about it. And as for you, miss, you shall either marry me or I'll drive this knife to the hilt until I find your life.'"

At that moment, Brown's son Fred happened to walk by.

The young lady begged for help.

Fred told Sherman to leave her alone.

Grant: *"Fred Brown quietly warned Sherman that if he attempted any violence, he would be taken care of. With an oath and threat, Sherman left them."*[182]

The violence was just starting. The small town of Lawrence, Kansas had grown into a nice place with a hotel, restaurants, and other businesses. They even had a town newspaper preaching abolitionism. That upset the border ruffians who threatened to burn the town to the ground.

The border ruffians did not hide their lust for violence.

In southern newspapers they promised to drive out the abolitionists by any means possible. *"We will continue to tar and feather, drown, lynch and hang every abolitionist who dares to pollute our soil."[183]*

These were very real threats. More dangerous men were sent to cause trouble in Kansas.

John Jr. would later describe, *"Early in the spring of 1856, Colonel Buford of Alabama arrived with a regiment of armed men, mostly from South Carolina and Georgia. They came with the openly declared purpose of making Kansas a slave state at all hazards. A company of these men was reported to us as encamped about two miles from our place."*

As the violence came closer and closer, Brown's sons worried about their families.

When Brown heard about the group of armed men camped just a few miles away, he decided to do a recon mission. In the past, he had done surveying work and still had all the equipment. That could be his cover to infiltrate the border ruffians' camp and learn their plans.

One day Brown took his surveying equipment over to the camp of Col. Buford's hired men. He calmly set up his equipment and pretended to survey property lines. No one bothered him. They figured he had been hired to do it.

What Brown heard, would chill his blood.

His son John described, *"Father took his surveyor's compass and four of my brothers, Owen, Fred, Salmon, and Oliver as chain carryers, ax men and markers. He found a section line that led through the camp of these men."*

"The Georgians talked freely. One who appeared to be the leader of the company said, 'We've come here to stay. We won't make no war on them as minds their own business; but all the abolitionists, such as them damned Browns over there, we're going to whip, drive out, or kill.'"[184]

His son Salmon described, *"The Border Ruffians never suspected us to be anything but friends, for only proslavery men got government jobs then, and surveyors were supposed to be government officers."*

"So they talked freely about their plans and one big fellow said, 'We came up here for self first and the South next. But one thing we will do before we leave, we'll clear out the damned Brown crowd."[185]

In Brown's own words, he described, *"I had heard that these men were coming to the cabin that my son and I were staying in to set fire to it and shoot us as we ran out. Now that was not proof enough for me, but I thought that I would satisfy myself that if they had committed murder in their hearts, I would be justified in killing them."*

"I was an old surveyor so I disguised myself and took men to carry the equipment. The lines not being run, I knew that as soon as they saw me, they would come out to find out where their lines would come."

"I kept looking through my instrument, making motions to the flag men to move either way, and at the same time I wrote every word they said. I ran my lines close to each man's house."

"The first man that came out, said, 'Is that my line, sir?'"

Brown: *"I cannot tell, I am running test lines. You have a fine country here, a great pity there are so many abolitionists in it."*

Reply: *"Yes but by God we will soon clean them out."*

Brown: *"I hear there are some bad men here by the name of Brown."*

Reply: *"Yes there are but by next Wednesday night, we shall kill them."*[186]

Brown kept listening and they kept talking. *"They said that Kansas must be a slave state at all costs to save Missouri from abolition. That both must stand or fall together. They did not hesitate to threaten that they would burn, kill, scalp and drive out the entire free state population of the territory if necessary."*[187]

They told Brown how William Sherman, Mr. Wilkinson and Mr. Doyle, had gone to Missouri to organize a group of border ruffians. That they planned to kill Brown and his sons in order to terrorize the rest of the free state settlers into leaving.[188]

William Sherman lived with his brother Henry Sherman. Their house was the local tavern.

Proslavery men would come, drink and plan their next move. Mr. Doyle and his two adult sons, age 20 and 22, often visited the Sherman's.

Mr. Doyle had been with the ruffians when Brown did his surveying recon. John Jr. had noticed Doyle went out of his way to travel *"a distance of nine miles"* to help the ruffians know the best ways to move through the woods and cross the river and creeks.[189]

This was a well organized criminal group.

William Sherman was a dangerous man. The three Doyle men were bad neighbors too.

Another Kansas settler named August Bondi later described, *"The Doyles had been slave hunters before they came to Kansas and had brought along two of their blood hounds."*

"William Sherman, a German from Oldenburg and a resident of Kansas since 1845, had amassed considerable property by robbing cattle droves and emigrant trains. He was a giant, 6'4 and had made it his pastime, with the Doyles, to break in the doors of free state settlers, frightening and insulting the families, or once in a while attacking and ill treating a man whom they encountered alone."[190]

Mr. Wilkinson was the mailman so he had the perfect cover for sending messages back and forth. He was also the first to know when free state settlers received mail.

Mr. Wilkinson had been elected to the Kansas territory legislature and voted for all the proslavery laws. He was also a bully.

Grant described how the neighbors saw him as *"The most evil looking man, who fearfully abused a nice wife, well liked by the neighbors."*[191]

Brown knew they were very violent. They had already threatened to attack the peaceful town of Lawrence, Kansas.

What happened next was later described by Kansas resident George Grant. *"When we heard that the border ruffians were threatening Lawrence, we immediately began to prepare."*

"*Fred Brown went to a store and bought some bars of lead, twenty or thirty pounds. The store was kept by Mr. Morse from Michigan, a quiet free state man living there with his two boys.*"

"*Fred brought the lead to my father's house on Sunday morning and my brother Henry and sister Mary spent the whole day making bullets.*"

"*As Fred was bringing this lead to our house, he passed by Henry Sherman's house. Several proslavery men, among them Doyle and his sons, William Sherman and others were sitting on the fence and asked what he was going to do with it. Fred said he was going to make bullets for free state guns.*"

"*They were very angry at his reply, as they knew the free state group was then preparing to go to Lawrence.*"

"*The next morning, after the group had started to go to Lawrence, a number of proslavery men, Wilkinson, Doyle, his two sons, and William Sherman, took a rope and went to the store owner's house. They said they were going to hang him for selling lead to the free state men. They frightened the man terribly but finally told him he must leave the country before 11:00AM or they would hang him. They then left, went to the Sherman's and went to drinking.*"

"*About 11:00AM some of them, half drunk, went back to Mr. Morse's and were going to kill him with an axe. His little boys, one was only nine years old, set up a violent crying and begged for their father's life.*"

"*They gave him until sundown to leave. He left everything and came at once to our house. He came carrying a blanket and leading his little boy by the hand.*"

"*When night came, he was so afraid that he would not stay in the house, but went out doors and slept on the prairie in the grass. For a few days he lay about in the brush, most of the time getting his meals at our house. He was then taken violently ill and died.*"

"While the free state group was gone to Lawrence, Henry Sherman came to my father's house and said, 'We have ordered Morse out of the country, and many others of the free state families have got to go.'"

"The general feeling among the free state people was terror, while the men were gone. We did not know at what moment the Georgia ruffians might come in and drive us all out."[192]

The group of men going to protect Lawrence included John Brown and his sons. They walked over thirty miles, in hopes of getting to Lawrence before the ruffians did.

They didn't make it in time. While they were on the way, the border ruffians attacked.

First thing the border ruffians destroyed was the printing press to stop the newspapers. They also destroyed the hotel, so no more settlers could come. After they had wrecked havoc they left. Maybe that would make the pesky abolitionists go home.

Southern newspapers reported on the violent attack: *"Today we have entered Lawrence with 'southern rights' inscribed upon our banner and not one damned abolitionist dared to fire a gun. This is the happiest day. We have entered that damned town, and taught the damned abolitionists a southern lesson that they will remember until the day they die. And now boys we will go in again and teach them that Kansas shall be ours."[193]*

The attack had the opposite effect. It made the people of Lawrence even more determined to stay and fight. Samuel Pomeroy was in charge of public safety for the town of Lawrence. He later described how the town had vainly hoped the government would protect them.

On the night of May 21, 1856, when the border ruffians came to attack, he told the residents to stand down. He described, *"I insisted, though our town was threatened with destruction, that we should give the government a fair opportunity to protect us. So we stood still and saw our printing presses and buildings madly destroyed. As the government gave no protection, the next morning, we resolved that every man who threatened our lives should be driven to Missouri or killed."[194]*

Brown was still on the road when he heard the news that the attack on Lawrence was over. The people of Lawrence sent word that anyone trying to help them should return home. Too much of their supplies had been destroyed. With very little food left, they didn't want any visitors.

Brown was upset that Lawrence didn't fight back. His group had walked for hours and hours only to find out that they would have to turn around and walk back. Discouraged at the news, Brown decided to camp for the night.

While he was trying to figure out what to do, more bad news arrived. The day after the attack on Lawrence, there had been another violent attack. Senator Sumner, the abolitionist in Congress, had been beaten almost to death by a proslavery Congressman.

As Salmon Brown later described, this news drove his father and the other men over the edge. *"A man named Gardner came to us with the news of the assault upon Senator Sumner. At that blow the men went crazy."*[195]

Then the last straw came. Mr. Doyle knocked at the Brown family's door. He knew that Brown and his sons were still on the road, so most of the men were gone from the house.

Doyle told the women, *"Tell your men that if they don't leave right off, we'll come back tomorrow and kill them."*[196]

That was a real threat. Word on the street was that Mr. Doyle had already murdered an abolitionist the day before.[197]

One of Brown's group, James Hanway, later described, *"While we were in camp on Middle Ottawa Creek in Franklin County, a young man, son of Mr. Grant, brought the news that certain proslavery citizens of the Pottawatomie had visited some of the free state families and threatened them with death and their property with destruction, if they did not leave the neighborhood by the following Sunday night."*[198]

There had always been a debate among abolitionists on whether peaceful protest was the only way or if they should fight back when attacked.

Brown had believed in peace until forced to respond to protect others. Now that multiple violent attacks had been made, how far would the enemy go?

At this point, Brown, his sons and several neighbors were still camped on the road on the way home. They had all the time in the world to discuss what to do. There was no law enforcement to protect them. They were on their own.

The neighbors felt that it was time to fight fire with fire. As Jason described, "*Father cooked for our group. While he was cooking breakfast, I heard him, Townsley and Weiner talking.*"

"*Townsley said, 'We expect to be butchered, every free state settler in our region.'*"

"*I heard father say, 'Something must be done now. We have got to defend our families and our neighbors as best we can. Something must be done to show these barbarians that we have rights too. That there are two sides to this thing and they cannot go on with impunity.'*"

Salmon Brown described, "*Williams knew exactly who the (bad) men were. He lived among them. Williams wrote down the names of the men whom, he said, it was necessary to pick off to prevent the utter destruction of the whole community. He handed the paper to father. We started back for Pottawatomie Creek which was the headquarters for proslavery men. We were looking to pick off men prominent in enforcing border ruffian laws.*"[199]

Brown believed that violence was necessary when the lives of his family and friends were in danger. So he decided to take a small group of men and leave the bigger group. He told the others to keep traveling home and they would see them later.

Then Brown and his group started walking for Pottawatomie Creek. It took some time to get there. His sons Salmon and Owen were with him along with other neighbors.

They went to several different houses and found the men who had been threatening the free state settlers.

They killed Mr. Wilkinson, the proslavery politician who had abused his wife. Ironically that very night, he had gone to bed telling his wife how the free state settlers would be attacked so brutally that none would be left by the following Sunday night.[200]

They killed William Sherman, the cattle thief who had threatened to kill the young lady with a knife. They were not able to kill his brother Henry Sherman because he had left to find missing cattle.

They killed the slavehunters, Mr. Doyle and his two adult sons, age 20 and 22. They did not hurt Mrs. Doyle or the younger son who was only 16.

Brown's men used knives to keep their actions as quiet as possible because he feared that using guns would awaken the neighbors.

The next morning, the sun rose on a dark scene. Neighbors found five bodies lying on the ground. The dead men had had such a reign of terror that some neighbors were only surprised they had not been killed sooner. A female neighbor (name unknown) described how they were well known in the area as *"brutes and bullies."*[201]

Another neighbor (who probably did not give his name due to fear of retaliation) described how desperate the community had felt. *"At the time the Pottawatomie Creek massacre occurred, it was approved by myself and hundreds of others. It was one of the stern, merciless necessities of the times."*

"The night it was done, I was but a few miles away, on guard, to protect from destruction the homes of free state men and their families who had been notified by these men and their allies to leave within a limited time or forfeit their lives and property. The women and children dared not sleep in the houses, and were hid away in the thickets. Something had to be done."[202]

Samuel Pomeroy, one of Lawrence's town leaders, described how he approved of Brown's violence. *"That one act struck terror into the hearts of our enemies. Those deaths saved a multitude of lives and was the cheapest sacrifice that could be offered."*[203]

Brown did not want revenge but only self-defense. *"Do not allow anyone to say I acted from revenge. What I do, I do for the cause of human liberty and because I regard it as necessary."*[204]

Another free state neighbor, August Bondi, described, *"Wilkinson was one of the few southerners who were able to read and write and who prided himself accordingly. He was a member of the Border Ruffian Legislature, and a principal leader in all attempts to hurt the free state men. Although he never directly participated in the murders and robberies, still it was well understood that he was always informed a short time before an invasion of Missourians was to occur."*

"On the very day of his death, he had tauntingly said to some free state men that in a few days the last of them would be either dead or out of the territory."

"In this he referred to the coming invasion of Cook at the head of an 250 armed mob from Bates County, Missouri who (came) about May 27 and plundered the whole region."[205]

That group got revenge on Brown's family. They burned his son's homes to the ground and destroyed their farms.

John Jr. described, *"I raised a company of riflemen from the free state settlers of Osawatomie and Pottawatomie Creek and marched to the defense of Lawrence in May 1856, but did not reach the place in time to save it from being burned by the Missourians. On this march, I was joined by three other groups and was chosen to be the command of the combined forces."*

"Returning to our homes, we found them burned to the ground by Buford's men from Alabama, who had marched in from Missouri on our rear."

"Our cattle and horses were driven off and dispersed, there only being three or four which we recovered. In the destruction of our houses, I lost my library of 400 books which I had been accumulating since I was sixteen."

"Since then we have, like David (in the Bible), had our dwelling with the serpents of the rocks and wild beasts of the wilderness; hid away from our enemies."

"We are not disheartened, though nearly destitute of food, clothing, and money. God has not given us over to the will of our enemies but has delivered them into our hand. We humbly trust God will still keep and deliver us. We feel assured that He who sees not as men see, does not lay the guilt of innocent blood to our charge."[206]

There was a Native American man who was helping the free state settlers. He had a beautiful home, which was always open to Brown on his travels back and forth. When Brown lost everything and was hungry, this friend helped him.

Brown described, *"I, with five sick and wounded sons and son in law, was obliged for some time to lie on the ground without shelter, our boots and clothes worn out, destitute of money and at times almost in a state of starvation and dependent on the charities of the Christian Indian and his wife."*

For that the border ruffians would burn his house to the ground. Brown described, *"John Jones is the most exemplary Christian Indian. He had a most valuable house full of good articles and stores. I saw the ruins of it after it was burned by the ruffians for suspecting he favored free state men."*

"I saw the burning of Osawatomie by 400 ruffians and of Franklin afterward by some 2,700 men. Deserted houses and cornfields were in almost every direction south of the Kansas River."[207]

The violence would continue.

Another settler O. C. Brown described, *"Hundreds of men have come from Missouri and the Southern and pauper crowd that live by plunder are hunting down the supposed murderers at Pottawatomie. But almost daily murders are committed near Westport and nothing done."*[208]

Another Kansas resident W. A. Phillips wrote, *"Proslavery parties stealthily prowled through the territory. Outrages were common. Murders were frequent, many passing secretly and unrecorded. Some of them only revealed by the discovery of some mouldering remains."*[209]

In the next few months, about 200 people died and hundreds of thousands of dollars of houses and farms were destroyed.[210]

During his time in Kansas, Brown had seen the dead body of abolitionist Thomas Barber in the street, with the wife and children weeping over it.

Brown may have helped Barber's widow without history recording it. History did record him helping the widow of a proslavery man. A proslavery newspaper wrote: *"At the sacking of Osawatomie, one of the most bitter proslavery men in Lykins County, Ed Timmons was killed."*

"Some time afterward, Brown stopped at the log house where Timmons had lived. His widow and children were there and in great destitution. He inquired into their wants, relived their distresses and supported them, until her friends in Missouri, who Brown told of the condition of Mrs. Timmon, had time to come and carry her to her former home."

"Mrs. Timmons fully appreciated the great kindness shown her but never learned that Brown was her benefactor."[211]

Yet seeing dead abolitionists lying in the street made Brown realize how dangerous life was on the frontier. He was determined not to end up shot down in broad daylight.

So when law enforcement came to arrest Brown and presented a warrant, Brown was ready. He pulled a gun and pointed it at the head of the lawman. He told them to leave. They left quickly.

After that, none of the proslavery men dared to approach Brown unless they had a large group for backup. Brown was actually able to go into Missouri and buy supplies, knowing no one would bother him.

Meanwhile, Brown's sons were hunted down. Law enforcement issued warrants for their arrest, even though John and Jason had nothing to do with the Pottawatomie murders.

John and Jason were warned that a mob was coming to arrest them. Jason did not want to wait around for the moment they would find him. So he decided to go meet them. He left by himself and quickly found the posse. They took him hostage, making him walk for hours to where they would hold him.

That gave Jason a lot of time to talk to them about the gospel. Some of them listened closely.

John was also found and arrested. His hands were tied behind his back so tightly that it cut off his circulation and left permanent marks on his wrists. He was also made to walk for miles to the place that they would be held.

What was going to happen to them? At the time, Kansas did not have a prison. They both wondered if they would be murdered.

Yet they were about to find out just how much the border ruffians feared their father. News of what Brown had done had traveled far and wide.

John later described, *"The day after we were taken to Paola, a proslavery man brought in and gave to the Missourians and Buford's men—who held our little company prisoners—a scrap of paper containing only these words:*

"I am aware that you hold my two sons." -John Brown

"The bearer of the paper said he brought it—knowing that his own life depended on its delivery."

"Jason and I occupied a room which contained a bed and a small lampstand. Two others also occupied the room as guards. The early part of the night had been spent by our guards playing cards at the little table. Jason was asleep."

"At about midnight, I was awakened by the sudden opening of the door and rushing in of a number of men with drawn bowie knives. Seizing the candle and saying 'Which are they?' they crowded around our bed with uplifted knives."

"Believing that our time had come, and wishing to save Jason from prolonged suffering, I opened his shirt, pointed at his heart, said 'Strike here.'"

"At this moment, the sudden and loud barking of dogs outside and a hurrying of steps on the porch, caused a most lively stampede of our assailants. This attack was ended without a blow."

"From Pottawatomie, father had become to slaveholders and their allies in Kansas, an omnipresent dread, filling them with forebodings of evil by day and haunting visions at night. That fear saved our lives."[212]

John and Jason were released unharmed.

Fred Brown was murdered at age 26. Just a few months after Pottawatomie happened, Fred had been helping protect the town of Osawatomie with a group of forty men. They were no match for hundreds of border ruffians armed with heavy weaponry and canons.

Early in the morning, when Fred got up to feed the horses, the border ruffians found him by himself. They shot him before he could draw his own pistol.

The man who pulled the trigger, Martin White, had been the person who had threatened the Brown family when they had first moved into the territory.

Brown had been close enough to hear the gunshot that killed his son. He came running and got there just in time to hold his son while the life drained out.

Something died in Brown's heart that day. He vowed never to be taken alive. After everything he had been through, he was not going to end up dead on the side of the road like so many other free state men.

Meanwhile, that same day, the town of Osawatomie was attacked. Brown tried to defend it, but lost the battle and had to retreat.

About a month later, Brown was invited to Lawrence, to meet with the free state leader Charles Robinson.

Several months prior, when the free state settlers had met together to form their own state government and had written the Topeka state constitution, they had also elected Charles Robinson as the lawful Kansas Governor. Robinson lived in Lawrence. During the previous attack, the border ruffians had burned his house down just to prove they would punish anyone who refused to submit to them.

BROWN SAVES LAWRENCE

Robinson had heard of Brown's violent reputation.

When they met in September 1856, he asked Brown to do something about the border ruffians. He wanted Brown to kill some of them and kidnap others to stop their reign of terror.

Brown refused. He was not the violent man everyone thought. He did not want to hurt anyone unless it was absolutely necessary.

Brown told Robinson, *"Do it yourself."*[213]

While Brown was in Lawrence for this meeting, the warning came that the border ruffians were about to attack again.

What happened next was later described by an eyewitness. (Because this was originally published at the time of the Civil War, he probably did not give his name for fear of retaliation.)

He wrote, *"I was up early on Sunday morning, went down to the river and bathed, came back to my tent on the west side of Lawrence, and busied myself in writing letters home. The number of men in town on that day was considerably less than usual, leaving Lawrence unprotected when news came that 2,800 Missourians were marching down."*

"We continued reading, writing, cooking, making bullets, cleaning guns and paid but little attention to rumors."

"Yet messenger after messenger arrived in town during the day, each one bringing additional news of the invading army. At 4:00pm we were compelled to believe these rumors for we saw the smoke of Franklin, a little town five miles south east of Lawrence, curling up towards heaven."

When the townspeople realized that Brown was there, they asked him to lead them. He got up on a box and made the following speech.

"Gentleman it is said that 2,500 Missourians are down at Franklin and that they will be here in two hours."

"You can see for yourselves the smoke they are making by setting fire to the houses in that town. Now is probably the last opportunity you will have of seeing a fight; so you had better do your best."

"If they should attack us, do not yell and make a great noise, but remain perfectly silent and still. Wait till they get within 25 yards of you, get a good focus, then fire. A great deal of powder, lead and very precious time is wasted by shooting too high. You had better aim at their legs than at their heads. It is this reason that I myself have so many times escaped, for if all the bullets aimed at me had hit me, I would have been full of holes."

The eyewitness continued, *"Having taught the arts of war, he started defense preparations. There were several forts, all manned with as many volunteers as could be spared."*

"Captain Brown was always on the alert, visiting every portion of the town and all fortifications in person, giving directions, exhorting every man to keep cool and do his duty. Among other preparations, a number of merchants went into their stores and brought out a large lot of pitchforks. Every man without a bayonet on his gun was furnished with a pitchfork."

"In the meantime, the invading army had left Franklin and were marching towards Lawrence. About 5:00pm their advance guard, consisting of 400 horsemen, crossed the Wakarusa and presented themselves in sight of town about 2 miles off. They halted and arrayed themselves for battle, fearing perhaps to come too close in range of Sharp's rifle balls."

"Brown's movement now was offensive, for he ordered out the forty Sharpe's riflemen from every part of town, marched them a half mile into the prairie and arranged them 3 paces apart in a line parallel with that of the enemy."

"They lay face down in the grass, awaiting the order to fire. While occupying this position, a gallant trooper from the enemy's side rode up about a half mile in advance of his comrades to recon; halting in the road, feasting his eyes."

"One of ours, a full mile off, fired at him. In 2 or 3 seconds, the ball struck in the road, at the horse's feet. The rider immediately wheeled about, and putting spurs to his horse, was soon out of the reach of even Sharpe's rifle balls."

"Brown now changed the position of his men to a rising piece of ground, about a quarter mile to the left, which overlooked a small cornfield of 8 or 10 acres, and there stationed them as before, with their faces to the ground."

"A simultaneous movement on the part of the enemy brought the two armies face to face, about a half mile apart, with the cornfield between them."

"It was now just approaching dusk. The sun went rapidly down. There was no light, even of the moon and stars."

"The distance now between the contending armies was to give to Sharpe's rifle balls, fired with precision, a deadly effect."

"In a few moments, the firing started. In the dark stillness of night, the continual flash, flash, flash, presented a terrible scene but sublimely beautiful."

"For fear that our few men would be surrounded in the darkness by the superior number of horsemen and cut to pieces, a 12 pound brass piece, under guard of 12 men, was sent to their assistance; but before it had arrived upon the ground, the foe had become panic stricken and fled."

"Several horses were found riderless. 400 strong, well armed and mounted men fled from 40 men."

"That night, T and I took our blankets and lay down with a stone for a pillow and clouds for a covering. We had been there a few moments, when Capt. Brown came along and said, 'With your permission I will be the third man to aid in defending this fortification tonight.'"

"He lay down by our side and told us of the trials and the wars he had passed through. That he had settled in Kansas with a large family, having six full grown sons, he had taken a claim in Lykins County."

"He was peacefully farming when the hordes of wild men came over from Missouri and took possession of all the ballot boxes, destroyed his corn, stole his horses, shot down his cattle, sheep and hogs."

"They repeatedly threatened to shoot him, hang him or burn him if he did not leave the territory."

"Told me that he held his son in his arms as he drew his last breath, and thought of the resemblance he bore to his mother. I thought in the anger of the moment, that had that been my son, I would have sworn forever to raise my voice and my arm against the measures and men who had hunted him to an untimely death."[214]

The town of Lawrence was saved that night from the attack. But Brown was running out of resources. The loss of the farms and livestock had left them broke. They needed resources to start over.

Brown knew that to continue the war for Kansas territory, he would have to raise support. He decided to travel back to the East Coast to visit his wife and the rest of the family. He also traveled to visit abolitionist groups to raise support in Massachusetts.

On February 18, 1857, Brown was invited to speak to the Massachusetts State Legislature about the violence in Kansas. He described seeing dead bodies of free state men in the street.

"I saw the body of Mr. Barber. I saw Mr. Parker, bruised and left for dead with his throat cut. I once saw three mangled bodies with twenty bullet wounds lying on the ground. One of these young men was my own son. I saw ruffians try to kill Dr. Graham. I saw several other free state men who were badly wounded by invaders of the territory. One of my sons was so wounded that he will be a cripple for life. I know numerous other people suffer like hardships."

"I saw the ruins of many free state men's houses together with thousands of dollars of grain burning and wasted. I know for much of the summer, travel through the territory was entirely cut off. Mails on different routes were entirely stopped. None dared move but groups of armed men."

They asked Brown what he needed. He replied that any money they could give would be a huge help.

"Whenever we heard in Kansas that the North was doing anything for us, we were encouraged and strengthened to go on."

He also asked for more people. *"We want good hard-working men, who fear God too much to fear anything human."*[215]

The Massachusetts State Legislature was very impressed by his speech. They did not give him any money, but local abolitionists groups did. Brown was able to raise significant money and supplies for Kansas. He came back with enough supplies to encourage the free state settlers to keep fighting.

He returned to Kansas, then made several more fundraising trips back and forth to the east coast.

While Brown was gone from Kansas for several months, there was a brutal attack.

Eli Snyder was a free state blacksmith who was friends with Brown. He lived right on the border of Kansas and Missouri. He had gone into Missouri and rescued a slave from his master. For that crime, the border ruffians sent a group to kill him.

Late one night, they attacked his house. Lots of bullets were fired, but Snyder was ready for them. He fought back with enough guns and ammo to drive them away. When they were unsuccessful in killing Synder, they got revenge on easier targets.

On May 19, 1858, the border ruffians kidnapped a group of eleven free state men. They ordered them to kneel. Then they fired. Five men died. Six escaped because they played dead. History would remember this as the Trading Post Massacre.

Brown was livid when he heard about it. Something more had to be done. Maybe it was time to go on the offensive.

HARPER'S FERRY REVOLT

For years, Brown had dreamed of leading a slave revolt to take down the whole evil system.

In 1831, a slave in Virginia, Nat Turner, was inspired by reading the Bible to lead a violent revolt. Other slaves followed him. By the time the dust cleared, 55 people were dead. As a result, southern states passed laws forbidding slaves from learning to read, lest they read the Bible and find out God wanted them to be free.

Brown had thought about Nat Turner for years. In 1837, long before the Kansas struggle, when he was living in Springfield Massachusetts, Brown had hosted a special guest at his house.

Frederick Douglas was a former slave and highly successful public speaker, leading abolitionist efforts. He had also become jaded with the peaceful protests that seemed to accomplish nothing. He had realized, *"Slavery is a system of brute force. It must be met with its own weapons."*[216]

He had argued the point with other abolitionists. He would later write, *"Speaking at an antislavery convention in Ohio, I expressed that slavery could only be destroyed by bloodshed. I was suddenly and sharply interrupted by my good friend Sojourner Truth with the question, 'Is God dead?'"*

"I answered, 'No. Because God is not dead, slavery can only end in blood.'"

"My quaint old sister was of the Garrison school of nonresistants and was shocked at my doctrine but she too became an advocate of the sword when the war for the Union was declared."[217]

Douglas traveled extensively. During his travels, he stayed at Brown's family home on the east coast. They had many discussions about the best way to end slavery. Brown told him how often he had thought about Nat Turner.

Brown pulled out a map and pointed at the mountains of Virginia. He talked about doing guerrilla warfare style raids.

He could help slaves run away to the mountains, then raid nearby plantations to get food and supplies.

Brown: *"Nat Turner with 50 men, held Virginia 5 weeks. The same number well organized and armed can shake the system out of the state. A few men in the right can overturn a king. Twenty men in the mountains could break slavery to pieces in two years."*[218]

"These mountains are the basis of my plan. God has given the strength of the hills to freedom. They were placed here for emancipation. They are full of natural forts, where one man for defense will be equal to a hundred for attack. They are full also of good hiding places where large numbers of brave men could be concealed and elude pursuit for a long time. I know these mountains well and could take a body of men into them and keep them there, despite all the efforts of Virginia to dislodge."

Brown's plan was *"to destroy the money value of slave property. That can only be done by rendering such property insecure. My plan is to take 25 well picked men, supply them arms and ammo and post them in squads of 5 on a line of 25 miles. The best of them shall go down to the fields from time to time and get the slaves to join them."*

"When 100 are properly drilled, they would run off the slaves in large numbers, retain the strong ones in the mountains and send the weak to the north."

Douglas disagreed and tried to convince Brown that his plan would fail. The first problem was food. How would they eat while living in the mountains?

Brown replied that they could take what they needed from local plantations.

Douglas asked what about slavehunters with bloodhounds?

Brown: *"They might attempt, but when we have whipped one squad, they would be careful how they pursued. The worst thing that could happen is dying and I'm willing to die."*[219]

Brown's heart was in the right place but he had no clue what he was doing. Still, he persisted, believing that he had to do something.

As the years passed, he changed his mind. He would meet again with Douglas. This time the plan was different.

Brown told Douglas about his idea of taking an armory in Virginia. He would barricade himself inside, wait for slaves to join him, then fight his way out. He felt that once the slaves heard what they were doing, they would rise up and join his revolt.

Douglas told him the idea would fail. *"That he was going into a perfect steel trap and would never get out alive."*

Brown thought that if he took some hostages, he would be able to escape. No one would shoot him.

Douglas again tried to warn Brown that the plan was doomed. *"I told him that Virginia would blow him sky high rather than that he should hold Harper's Ferry. We spent most of Saturday and Sunday in this debate. He for striking a blow, which should instantly rouse the country. I for the policy of gradually drawing off slaves to the mountains as he first suggested."*[220]

Brown still insisted on following his plan.

Why?

The answer might have come from something he had told a friend. During the time he was traveling on the east coast to raise funds for the fight in Kansas, there was a price on his head. So when he stayed with friends, he kept his weapons close. Every night he carefully cleaned his guns, to be ready in case someone came to kill him. He told the lady of the house, *"If you hear a noise at night, put the baby under the pillow. I should hate to spoil these carpets but you know I cannot be taken alive."*[221]

That was a much different answer than what Brown had said when friends in Kansas tried to warn him how *"Missourians were determined, sooner or later, to take his scalp."*

At that time, Brown's reply had been *"The angel of The Lord will camp round about me (Psalms 34:7)."*[222]

After all the violence in Kansas, had Brown changed his mind and felt his time was running out? Did he want to die in a blaze of glory? Was he afraid that he was going to be gunned down in the streets, and instead wanted to choose how he died? Maybe that's why he decided to attack Harper's Ferry.

Meanwhile, God was trying to warn him to turn back from his plan. When Brown did not listen to Douglas, God sent other people to warn him. One of them was Harriet Tubman.

Brown had first met Harriet while traveling in Canada. Later he met with her again while traveling on the east coast. He was very impressed, calling her *"The best and bravest."*[223]

She was encouraged by everything he was doing to fight the evil system. She helped him raise funds to continue the efforts but she was warned by God in a dream about his plans.

In the dream Harriet *"was in a wilderness sort of place, full of rocks and bushes."* Then *"a snake raised its head among the rocks. As it did so, it became the head of an old man with a long white beard. He gazed at her, wishful as if he was going to speak. Then two other heads rose up beside him, younger than he."*

As she wondered what they wanted to tell her, *"A great crowd of men rushed in and struck down the younger heads, then the head of the old man."*[224]

That dream made no sense to her until she met Brown soon after. She recognized his face from the dream.

The dream was a warning from God that would come true. Brown and two of his sons would strike a blow like a snake then be struck down during the raid on Harper's Ferry. But before Brown failed at that revolt, he succeeded in something different.

After that dark night on Pottawatomie Creek, Brown's violent reputation had spread far and wide. It reached someone in Missouri who needed help.

One day in December of 1858, while Brown was in Kansas, a slave named Jim knocked at his door.

He had come all the way from Missouri to ask for help. His family was about to be sold far away. Would Brown rescue them?

That was a big favor to ask in the middle of winter. How would Brown get an entire family of eleven people to safety across hundreds of miles covered in snow?

At the time, Brown was preparing for the Harper's Ferry battle but he remembered one of his favorite Bible verses in Proverbs 21:13 (NOG). *"Whoever shuts his ear to the cry of the poor will call and not be answered."*

Brown took a few friends and supplies, went to the plantation and rescued the man's family. Then they started for Canada in a horse drawn wagon. The journey took several weeks. Along the way, they were given food and supplies by people on the Underground Railroad.

Word traveled fast. Slave catchers were sent to capture them. But they were nervous about approaching Brown, believing the stories about his violent reputation.

After everything he had been through, Brown realized that he could safely travel in slave territory because people feared him. No one person would approach him by themselves, and it would take too much time to put together a large group. *"It is perfectly understood that I will not be taken alive. No little handful of men would undertake it and a large group cannot be got together in season."*[225]

Brown's reputation was so powerful that the armed posse of slave-catchers were terrified at approaching Brown and his small group.

By the time they caught up to him, Brown had divided his team into different groups. Some of the men had gone to get supplies. Others were waiting in a cabin for the men to return with supplies.

One of the men (name unknown) would later describe, *"There had been heavy rains which produced flood waters. One day as one of our men walked out of the cabin to see if the waters had subsided, eight of the marshal's men came upon him suddenly. They asked if he had seen any negroes. He told them to come with him and he would show them some."*

"He took them to the cabin where he had left his rifle. Then he pointed his rifle at the leader and told him to surrender, which he did at once. The other men put spurs to their horses and rode off as fast as possible."

"We waited at the cabin three days. At last, our supplies arrived and we were joined by young men from Kansas who had come to help us. We then started on the journey. A short distance from our road was Muddy Creek where the marshal, supposing our group would pass that way, stationed himself on the opposite side of the creek with 80 armed men. He had made careful preparations, knowing it was no joke to attack Brown."

"We had only 23 men with us. Brown put them in two columns in front of the wagons and said, 'Now go straight at them. They'll run.'"

"We marched towards the creek and barely entered the water when the marshal mounted his horse and rode off quickly. His men followed as fast as possible."

"The scene was ridiculous. Some horses were quickly mounted by two men. One man grabbed the tail of the horse, trying to leap on while the rider was putting spurs into his sides so he went flying through the air. Our men on horseback followed them and took five prisoners. Meanwhile Brown and the rest of the group got the wagons through the creek using ropes."

"When we continued our journey, Brown didn't want the five prisoners to mount their horses lest they escape and bring more men to attack us. So he told them they must walk but he would walk with them as he meant no unkindness. They went on together, he talking with them all the way on the wickedness of slavery. He kept them with us all night. In the morning, he told them they could walk back. Their horses were kept for the safety of our group lest they return home too quickly. The captured horses were given to the Kansas young men who had walked so far to help us."[226]

When the hostages got back home, they told everyone about what had happened. There were some funny stories. Their families were amused to hear that during their long night in captivity they had often cursed in frustration.

Brown had heard them and replied, *"Gentleman, you do very wrong to take the Lord's name in vain. If there is a God, you can gain nothing by such profanity. If there is no God, how foolish to ask God's curses on anything!"*[227]

Several weeks later, Brown's team made it safely to Canada. They had saved the lives of eleven people. Plus, there was a new addition. One of the women was pregnant and had given birth to a baby they named John Brown. Once again Brown had succeeded at what he did best, running the Underground Railroad.

Brown returned to Kansas to help the free state settlers. Then he continued working on his bigger plan, recruiting several people to help him. Once he had a team, he went to the South and rented a farmhouse in Maryland near Harper's Ferry.

Photo of a train crossing the bridge over the Potomac River at Harper's Ferry. Photo taken in 1898 by Benjamin Lloyd Singley.

In 1799, the federal government began developing Harper's Ferry as a place to make and store weapons. It was a secure location surrounded by water and only accessible by two bridges. There were several brick buildings there that could easily block incoming bullets. Brown chose that location because it was full of weapons with limited access points. A few men could easily hold it.

Osborne Anderson was one of five black men who helped Brown plan the revolt. According to Anderson, they spent a year preparing. They lived on the Maryland farm for months, doing recon, gathering supplies, and preparing weapons.

They also prayed for freedom. As Anderson later described, *"Every morning, he called the family around, read from his Bible and prayed the most fervent and touching prayers for the oppressed. I never heard John Brown pray without praying for deliverance for slaves."[228]*

Anderson also wrote, *"The idea for Harper's Ferry came from the work of Moses who disturbed the comfort of Pharaohs with 'Thus says the Lord, Let My people go! (Exodus 9:1).'"*

"Coming down through the nations, it was been proclaimed by free men and slaves. There is an unbroken chain of purpose from Moses to Denmark Vesey, Nat Turner, Madison Washington (Creole ship revolt) to John Brown."[229]

The five black men who joined Brown were Osborne Anderson, John Copeland, Shields Green, Lewis Leary and Dangerfield Newby.

Dangerfield Newby was a highly skilled blacksmith. While he was a free man, his wife and several children were slaves. He had tried to buy their freedom but his money was rejected, making him desperate to save his family.

Shields Green had grown up as a slave in Charleston, South Carolina.

When he escaped to freedom, he never forgot how evil the system was. He did not want anyone else to suffer what he had. He was recruited by Frederick Douglas to help Brown.

The irony is that Douglas had been asked by the black community to join the raid.[230] Douglas refused, but sent Green instead.

John Copeland was a highly educated college student who had studied at Oberlin after the Lane Rebels had turned it into another station on the Underground Railroad. He had been active in helping slaves escape yet wanted to do more to destroy the evil system. He had been recruited by his uncle Lewis Leary.

Lewis Leary was a skilled tradesman and family man, living near Oberlin College. He did not have to sacrifice everything for others but he was willing to give his life. He said, *"I'm ready to die! I only ask that when I have given my life to free others, my own wife and dear little daughter shall never know want."*[231]

They all believed the same thing. That freedom was God's will. Someone just had to do something about it.

After months of preparation, the time finally came. At 8:00pm on the night of October 16, 1859, Brown told them it was time.

During the mission, he wanted them to avoid violence as much as possible. *"You all know how dear life is to you. Do not take the life of anyone if you can possibly avoid it."*[232]

With those words, Brown sent them out to start the revolt.

Late at night when the town was sleeping, they silently moved into position.

First, they cut the telegraph wires to stop communications. Then they extinguished the street lights. Then they took the armory.

Harper's Ferry was actually several different buildings. Brown had his men attack in small groups at different areas to maximize their advantage.

Some men were sent to attack the armory and take captive the watchmen.

Other men were stationed on the bridges to block access points to the town and stop anyone from coming. The rest were assigned to hold specific buildings to maximize their viewpoints, provide cover and the ability for Brown to hold positions.

Photo of the brick building that John Brown chose to stand
his ground.

Brown took the fire engine brick building. There were only a few men guarding it. They were easily overpowered and tied up. Then he sent Anderson with a group to take hostages in the town.

Anderson's group was quick and effective. They had done enough research to know exactly how many residents lived there and where the slaves lived.

The first place they went was the home of George Washington's relative, Lewis; a very well-known slaveowner.

Anderson's team woke him up in the middle of the night, made him get dressed and come to the armory with a number of his slaves.

Lewis was very upset at the inconvenience but had no choice and obeyed orders.

This was a brilliant move. The optics of George Washington who had fought for freedom, having a family who refused freedom to others, showed the nation the hypocrisy of the evil system.

Anderson's team also needed human shields to stop law enforcement from attacking.

Anderson loved the irony of getting to take control of someone who was used to controlling others. He later wrote, *"Being a colored man, and that colored men were only things in the South, it was proper the South be taught a lesson."*[233]

He also wrote that the slaves were thrilled to hear the news.

Anderson described that there were five men with him including Green and Leary. *"On the road, we met some colored men, to whom we made known our purpose. They immediately agreed to join us. They said they had been long waiting for an opportunity of the kind. Stevens asked them to go around among the colored people and circulate the news. The result was that many colored men gathered to the action."*

"One old colored lady, at whose house we stopped, a little way from the town, had a good time over the message we took her. This liberating the slaves was the very thing she had prayed for and dreamed about. Her heart was full of rejoicing over the fulfillment of a prophecy which had been her faith for long years."[234]

Brown had figured that hostages were the only way he would be able to walk out of there alive. It was the only way to make law enforcement hold their fire. By the end of the night, they had dozens of hostages all crammed into a small brick building.

Late that night, the train came through the town. Brown stopped it and held the conductor hostage for several hours. Then he let it go. The people on the train had no idea what was happening, so as the train moved on, they wrote notes and dropped it out the windows, trying to call for help.

All through the night, Brown's team held Harper's Ferry.

The next morning, several hours passed before the town realized something was wrong.

The town was very confused by all the commotion. They thought it was a labor strike. That some disgruntled railroad workers were taking control of the bridges to demand better working conditions. No one thought it was a slave revolt.

Brown was still barricaded in the armory with the hostages and some of his men. The plan was working. But there was something he didn't plan for. He had a soft heart.

Brown knew he needed to leave and disappear into the mountains. But he delayed and waited too long, because the hostages did not want to walk all the way to the mountains. He listened to their complaining and worried more about their comfort than his own safety.

That was the fatal mistake. He stayed too long in the same place, giving General Robert E. Lee time to bring the U.S. Marines.

The marines made a heavy assault on the armory. Bullets flew in all directions. When the marines breached open the door and charged into the armory, Brown could have easily killed them. But he didn't want to hurt the military who were only doing their job. So he held his fire to save their lives.

The military quickly took control, freeing the hostages and arresting him.

Two of his sons died that day.

Watson Brown had been only 24 years old when he left his wife and toddler son to join the revolt. Believing that slavery was so evil, any sacrifice against it was worth it, he had written to his wife about the horrible things he had seen while living in Virginia and preparing for the revolt.

He described how one of the black men on their team *"has a wife and seven children in slavery."* How just during the time they were preparing for the raid, there had been *"five murders"* of slaves.

"There was a slave near here whose wife was sold south the other day. He was found in Thomas Kennedy's orchard dead the next morning. I cannot come home as long as such things are done. If we die, you must live to be a mother to our little son."[235]

Watson was shot while defending the armory.

Anderson described, *"After an hour's hard fighting, when the enemy were blocking the avenues of escape, Brown sent out his son Watson with a flag of truce. No respect was paid to it. He was shot and wounded severely. He returned to the engine house and fought bravely after that for an hour and a half when he received a mortal wound."*[236]

Watson died from the bullet wound within a few minutes.

Brown's youngest son, Oliver, also died at the armory. He was only 19 years old and married, making his wife a widow.

Of the five black men on the team, two of them were killed in battle.

Dangerfield Newby, the blacksmith, was killed by a sniper.

Anderson described how they had been holding the arsenal when *"he was shot through the head by a person who took aim at him from a brick store window on the opposite side of the street. Newby was shot twice. At the first shot he fell on his side and returned fire. As he lay, a second shot was fired and entered his head. He died at my side."*[237]

Lewis Leary also died fighting to his last breath. According to Anderson, Leary had been positioned with Kagi, a close friend of Brown who had helped him during the Kansas struggles. With them was John Copeland and *"three colored men from the neighborhood. At an early hour, Kagi saw from his position the danger in remaining. He told Brown to leave."*[238]

When Brown delayed, Leary and Copeland suffered a brutal assault on their position. Their small group of six men held a building against hundreds of attackers.

Once the attackers *"battered down"* the front door, Brown's team *"were forced to retreat out the back way, fighting the whole time."*

Anderson described, *"They were pursued to the river. It being shallow, they waded out to a rock, midway and made a stand being completely hemmed in front and rear."*

"Five hundred shots were fired at them. They would not surrender into the hands of the enemy but kept on fighting until everyone was killed except John Copeland. Seeing he could do no more and all his associates were murdered, he allowed himself to be captured. Of the men shot on the rocks, some were slaves and they suffered death before they would desert their companions."[239]

John Copeland and Shields Green were put on trial, sentenced to death and hanged.

Of the five black men who had helped to plan Harper's Ferry, Anderson was the only one who escaped. He was posted at an outside position where he could see Brown at the other building. Anderson stood his ground until he saw Brown in cuffs. Then he headed back to the safe house where they had stashed supplies.

The house had been raided. All their supplies were taken. So Anderson went to another safe house, a nearby schoolhouse where they had stashed weapons.

No food was left there either. So Anderson went to the mountains, knowing it was not safe to stay there. For the next two days, he tried to survive without food. He kept moving in the mountains until he was able to find a cornfield. He stuffed his pockets with as much corn as he could and kept moving. Then he traveled at night and slept during the day. Eventually he made his way to a friend's house.

While the friend was giving him food, law enforcement knocked at the door. Anderson quickly dashed out the back just in time to escape. He made it safely to Canada and lived to publish an eyewitness account of what had happened.

Owen Brown was the only one of Brown's sons who survived Harper's Ferry, because he was able to escape to the mountains. He had been left with some other men to guard the weapons and supplies at the schoolhouse. When the revolt failed, they took as much supplies as they could carry with them and hid in the mountains. When they ran out of food, the other men went back to the city to look for food. They were promptly arrested.

Owen stayed in the mountains, surviving on wild plants. He continued traveling for weeks, walking all the way from Virginia back to safety in Ohio.

They had made the right decision to leave the schoolhouse. Law enforcement would raid the schoolhouse and find the weapons they had prepared. The authorities were surprised at how many guns they had. According to records just part of their supplies included:

102 Sharpe's rifles

13,000 Sharpe's cartridges

160 Sharpe's primers

12 reams cartridge paper

10 kegs gunpowder

12 pistols

56 powder for pistols

12 swords

483 pikes

150 broken handles for pikes

55 bayonets

14 pounds lead balls

16 picks

40 shovels with railroad bill for dozens more

1 pocket map of Kentucky

1 pocket map of Delaware

2 yards cotton flannel

1 pair cloth pants

1 pair linen pants

50 leather water caps

625 envelopes

21 lead pencils

3 steel pens

5 inkstands

47 small blank books.[240]

When the news media heard Brown was in jail, they were eager to talk to him. They came to the jail and asked for interviews.

Robert E. Lee was in charge of security, so he asked Brown if the media was bothering him and offered to kick them out.

Brown wanted to talk to the media.

For hours, Brown preached to the news media on why slavery was evil. Proslavery newspapers would print his words in full, giving him the biggest platform he had ever had.

It came with a high price. Brown was put on trial and found guilty of treason.

At the trial, Brown gave a powerful speech that would be printed in the newspapers and touch many hearts. He talked about how if he had done something for the rich and powerful, they would have praised him. They would have rewarded him. But they were punishing him simply for trying to help the powerless.

"This court acknowledges the validity of God's law. The Bible teaches me that all things I want men to do to me, I should do to them. It teaches me to remember them that are in bonds as bound with them (Hebrews 13:3). I tried to follow those instructions."

"Now if I must sacrifice my life for justice and mingle my blood with the blood of millions in this slave country whose rights are disregarded by wicked and cruel laws, I say let it be done."[241]

After hearing that speech, the court sentenced him to death by hanging. The last few days of his life, he sat in jail and wrote letters to family and friends. He told them not to grieve for him but trust God to change the nation.

He wrote, *"I look forward to other changes to take place in God's time."*[242]

"Do not grieve on my account. As I trust my life has not been thrown away so I also trust my death shall not be in vain. God can make it to be a thousand times more value to His cause than all the service that I have rendered during my life."[243]

"I feel as happy as Paul did when he lay in prison. He knew that if they killed him, it would greatly advance the cause of Christ."[244]

"As I believe most firmly that God reigns, I cannot believe that any thing I have done, suffered or may yet suffer, will be lost to the cause of God or humanity."[245]

Brown's wife came to visit him at the jail. He told her to trust God to make all things work together for good.

While he was in jail, there were several proslavery pastors that came to pray with him.

Brown was disgusted at how they could hold the Bible in their hands while denying the truth. He refused to pray with them because *"there are no ministers of Christ here. These ministers who profess to be Christian, and hold slaves or advocate slavery, I cannot abide them."*

"My knees will not bend in prayer with them while their hands are stained with the blood of souls."[246]

Brown was executed on December 2, 1859.

In the days that followed, six of his men (four white and two black) were also executed for their bravery.

John Brown leaving the jail. Artist is Thomas Hovenden
(1840-1895). Created in 1884.

Virginia Soldiers at John Brown's execution. John Wilkes
Booth is standing to the left of the soldier with the goatee.
Photographed by Lewis Graham Dinkle (1829-1906).

Months later, on January 29, 1861, Kansas won the battle and was admitted as a free state.

Anderson was thrilled when it happened. Looking back on Harper's Ferry, he published a memoir so that future generations would not forget the sacrifice for their freedom. He wrote, *"Today Kansas is free and owes that to John Brown more than any other man."[247]*

The free state settlers chosen capital of Topeka became the Kansas capital. Charles Robinson would serve as the lawful governor of Kansas, just as he had been elected.

The proslavery side would get revenge. During the Civil War, on August 21, 1862, the border ruffians destroyed the town of Lawrence. Dozens of people were killed. But the town would be rebuilt and still stands today.

Brown's wife, Mary, lived to age 68, finally dying in 1884.

Brown's second wife (Mary Ann) with their children

Brown's sons and daughters would remain close friends for the rest of their lives. Owen, Ruth, Jason and their families moved to Pasadena, California. There they lived the rest of their lives together. They were well known in the community with newspaper reporters coming to interview them about the history they had lived.

John Jr. remained in Ohio with his wife and children. The rest of the family would do the best they could with what little they had left.

Brown's life would inspire many others, including someone who wrote a song called John Brown's Body.

Today that song is sung as The Battle Hymn of the Republic.

Fifty years after Brown's death, on Dec 5, 1909, a black pastor gave a powerful speech to honor his memory.

More than many people, Frances knew how precious freedom is because he had been born and raised under the evil system of slavery.

The Civil War gave him the chance to escape.

When Congress passed the Thirteenth, Fourteenth, and Fifteenth Amendments destroying slavery and recognizing that former slaves had citizenship and voting rights, Frances was finally able to pursue his dreams.

With his new freedom, he became a pastor. He preached many powerful sermons that touched people.

On December 5, 1909, he preached a special church service to honor Brown's memory. That night he talked about Psalms 127:1 (NASB): *"Unless the LORD builds a house, They who build it labor in vain; Unless the LORD guards a city, The watchman stays awake in vain."*

He said, *"It is important for us to remember this and hold on to God. To make His Word, the guide of our lives."*

"We may think that we can get along without God, that we can work out the problem of our elevation without him, but we are mistaken. Let us live to the glory of God and train our children to do the same. This is what John Brown did and what we must do if we are to come out all right."

"Out of the darkness and seeming triumph of oppression and injustice, there came the Emancipation Proclamation and great Constitutional Amendments."

"Be assured God did not strike the shackles from your limbs and lift you to the plane of citizenship that he might desert you and leave you in the hands of your enemies. The same power that was with you in the dark days of slavery, and that stood behind you when the great amendments were being put through, will continue to be with you to the end."

"It was the power of God working through human agency that brought about emancipation and lifted you to citizenship and the sacred right of the ballot. Let us remember what God has wrought since the raid on Harper's Ferry and rejoice and give thanksgiving to Him."[248]

(More stories coming in Troublemakers Volume 2.......)

Bibliography

Abbott, Richard H. *Cobbler in Congress; the Life of Henry Wilson, 1812-1875.* Lexington: University Press of Kentucky, 1972.

Abelove, Henry. "Jonathan Edward's Letter of Invitation to George White-field." *The William and Mary Quarterly* 29, no. 3 (July 1972): 487-89. JSTOR.

Adams, Alice Dana. *The Neglected Period of Anti-Slavery in America (1808-1831).* Google Books. Boston: Ginn & Company, 1908.

Addresses on the Death of Hon. Owen Lovejoy: Delivered in the Senate and House of Representatives, on Monday, March 28, 1864. Google Books. Washington: Gov Printing Office, 1864.

Aldridge, Alfred. "George Whitefield's Georgia Controversies." *The Journal of Southern History* 9, no. 3 (August 1943): 357-80. JSTOR.

Anderson, Osborne P. *A Voice from Harper's Ferry,* Boston: Self-Published. 1861. Archive.org.

Aptheker, Herbert. *A Documentary History of the Negro People in the United States.* Vol. I. New York: Citadel press, 1971.

Aptheker, Herbert. *American Negro Slave Revolts.* New York: International Publishers, 1993.

Ashbury, Francis. *Journal of the Rev. Francis Asbury Bishop of The Methodist Episcopal Church.* Vol. 1-3. New York: Bangs and Mason, 1821. Archive.org.

Babb, Tara Leigh. *Without A Few Negroes: George Whitefield, James Haber-sham and Bethesda Orphan House in the Story of Legalizing Slavery in Colonial Georgia.* Master's thesis, University of South Carolina, 2013. South Carolina: Scholar Commons, 2013.

Baine, Rodney. "The Prison Death of Robert Castell and Its Effect on the Founding of Georgia." *The Georgia Historical Quarterly* 73, no. 1 (Spring 1989): 67-78. JSTOR.

Ball, Charles. *Fifty Years in Chains,* Google Books. New York: H. Dayton, 1859.

Bancroft, George. *History of the United States of America, from the discovery of the continent.* Google Books. Vol. 1. New York: Appleton, 1888.

Bangs, Nathan. *The life of the Rev. Freeborn Garrettson,* New York: J. Emory and B. Waugh for the Methodist Episcopal Church, 1829.

Beecher, Charles, Charles C. Burleigh, Susan C. Cabot, Maria Weston Chapman, E. L. Follen, Octavius Brooks Frothingham, Thomas Wentworth Storrow Higginson, et al. *Anti-Slavery Tracts No 18: The Fugitive Slave Law and Its Victims.* Kindle Edition. New York: American Anti-Slavery Society, 1856.

Belcher, Joseph. *George Whitefield: A Biography, with Special Reference to His Labors in America.* New York: American Tract Society, 1857. Archive.org.

Bennett, Lerone. *Before the Mayflower: a History of Black America.* Harmonds-worth, Middlesex: Penguin Books, 1987.

Blackett, R. J. M. "Fugitive Slaves in Britian: The Odyssey of William and Ellen Craft." *Journal of American Studies* 12, no. 1 (April 1978): 41–62.

Bradford, Sarah. *Harriet Tubman, the Moses of Her People.* New York: Lock-wood, 1886. Archive.org.

Brewster, Rebekah. *Christians That Fought Slavery,* Published June 4, 2023.

Bowditch, Vincent Yardley, and Henry I. Bowditch. *Life and correspondence of Henry Ingersoll Bowditch.* Vol. 2. Boston: Houghton, Mifflin and Co., 1902.

Campbell, Stanley W. *The Slave Catchers; Enforcement of the Fugitive Slave Law, 1850-1860.* Chapel Hill: University of North Carolina Press, 1970.

Cartwright, Peter, and W. P. Strickland. *Autobiography of Peter Cartwright: The Backwoods Preacher.* New York: Carlton & Porter, 1857. Google Books.

Cate, Margaret. "Fort Frederica and the Battle of Bloody Marsh." *The Georgia Historical Quarterly* 27, no. 2 (1943): 111-74. JSTOR.

Chandler, William E., and Hiram Americus Tuttle. *The Statue of John P. Hale presented to the State of New Hampshire by William E. Chandler of Concord. An Account of the Unveiling Ceremonies on August 3, 1892.* Concord, NH: Republican Press Association, 1892. Library of Congress.

Chapman, Maria Weston. *Right and Wrong in Massachusetts.* Dow & Jackson, 1839.

Chilcote, Paul Wesley. *John Wesley and the Women Preachers of Early Methodism.* Scarecrow Press, 1991.

Christie, John W. "Newly Discovered Letters of George Whitefield." *Journal of the Presbyterian Historical Society* XXXII, no. 2 (June 1954).

Clinton, Catherine. "Crossroads at Harper's Ferry." In *Harriet Tubman: The Road to Freedom*, 124-39. Boston, MA: Little, Brown, 2004.

Coffin, Joshua. *An Account of Some of the Principal Slave Insurrections, in the United States and Elsewhere, During the Last Two Centuries.* Archive.org. New York: American Antislavery Society, 1860.

Coffin, Levi. *Reminiscences of Levi Coffin,* Google Books. Cincinnati: Clarke, 1880.

Collision, Gary. "This Flagitious Offense." *New England Quarterly* 68, no. 4 (December 1995): 609–25.

Collison, Gary. *Shadrach Minkins: From Fugitive Slave to Citizen.* Cambridge, MA: Harvard University Press, 1997.

Copley, Esther. *A History of Slavery, and its Abolition.* London: Houlston & Stoneman, 1839.

Cousins, Norman. *In God We Trust: The Religious Beliefs and Ideas of the American Founding Fathers.* New York: Harper & Brother Publishers, 1958.

Craft, William, and Ellen Craft. *Running a Thousand Miles for Freedom.* Archive.org. London: William Tweedie, 1860.

Franklin, Benjamin. *The Autobiography of Ben Franklin.* Edited by Charles W. Elliot. New York: P.F. Collier & Son, 1909. Kindle Edition.

Franklin, Benjamin, and Jared Sparks. *The life of Benjamin Franklin.* Boston: Whittemore, 1856.

Franklin, Benjamin. *Memoirs of the life and writings of Benjamin Franklin.* Edited by William Temple Franklin. Vol. 1. London: Printed for Henry Colburn, 1818.

Gledstone, James Paterson. *The Life and Travels of George Whitefield.* London: Longmans, Green, 1871. Google Books.

Goodell, William. *Slavery and Anti-Slavery; a History of the Great Struggle in Both Hemispheres.* New York: William Goodell, 1855. Google Books.

Dillon, Merton L. *Slavery Attacked.* Baton Rouge: Louisiana State Univ. Press, 1990.

Dodd, William Edward, and Jesse Macy. *The Days of the Cotton Kingdom.* Google Books. New Haven: Yale University Press, 1919.

Doolittle, Robinson, *Kansas,* Boston Mass.: Crosby, Nichols, 1857. Archive.org.

Douglass, Frederick, and John Bright. *The Life and Times of Frederick Douglass.* Christian Age Office, 1882. Google Books.

Du Bois W. E. *Souls of Black Folk.* Kindle Edition by Project Gutenberg. Cambridge, Massachusetts: University Press, 1903.

Du Bois W. E. *The Suppression of the African Slave Trade to the United States of America 1638-1870.* Kindle Edition by Project Gutenberg. Vol. I. New York: Harvard Historical Studies, 1896.

Fairchild, James Harris. *The Underground Railroad.* Google Books. Cleveland, OH: Western Reserve Historical Society, 1895.

Federer, William J. *America's God and Country: Encyclopedia of Quotations.* Coppell, TX: Fame, 1994.

Franklin, John Hope, and Loren Schweninger. *Runaway Slaves: Rebels on the Plantation.* New York: Oxford University Press, 1999.

Garrison, Wendell. *William Lloyd Garrison 1805-1879: the Story of His Life as Told by His Children.* Vol. 1–4. Houghton Mifflin, 1889.

Gates, Henry Louis. *Life upon These Shores: Looking at African American History, 1513-2008.* New York: Alfred A. Knopf, 2011.

Gledstone, James Paterson. *The Life and Travels of George Whitefield.* London: Longmans, Green, 1871. Google Books.

Goodell, William. *Slavery and Anti-Slavery; a History of the Great Struggle in Both Hemispheres.* New York: William Goodell, 1855. Google Books.

Greene, Lorenzo J. *The Negro in Colonial New England.* New York: Atheneum, 1968.

Hagedorn, Ann. *Beyond the River: The Untold Story of the Heroes of the Underground Railroad.* New York: Simon & Schuster, 2002.

Hahn, Steven C. *Life and Times of Mary Musgrove.* Florida: University Press of Florida, 2012.

Hale, John P. *Speech of John P. Hale Upon Slavery Resolution in the House of Representatives, Thursday June 25, 1846.* Library of Congress. www.loc.gov.

Hale, John P. *Speech of John P. Hale Delivered in the U.S. Senate on January 19 and 21, 1858.* Archive.org.

Hale, John P. *Speech of John P. Hale on The Territorial Question. Delivered in the Senate Tuesday March 19, 1850.* Archive.org.

Hall, Daniel. *Addresses Commerative of Abraham Lincoln and John P. Hale.* Google Books. Concord, NH: Republican Press Association, 1892.

Hamilton, James Albert. *Negro Suffrage and Congressional representation.* Www.archive.org. New York: Winthrop Press, 1910.

Hanke, Lewis. *The Spanish Struggle for Justice in the Conquest of America.* Philadelphia: University of Pennsylvania Press, 1949.

Hanke, Lewis. "Free Speech In Sixteenth Century Spanish America." *Hispanic American Historical Review* 26, no. 2 (May 1943): 135–49.

Helps, Arthur. *The Spanish Conquest in America: and its Relation to the History of Slavery and to the Government of Colonies.* Google Books. Vol. 1–4. London: J. W. Parker and Son, 1855.

Henry, Stuart Clark. *George Whitefield: Wayfaring Witness.* New York: Abingdon Press, 1957.

Hirschfeld, Fritz. *George Washington and Slavery.* Columbia: University of Missouri Press, 1997.

Hoffman, Michael A. *They Were White and They Were Slaves the Untold History of the Enslavement of Whites in Early America.* Dresden, N.Y: Wiswell Ruffin House, 1992.

Holt, Rosa Belle, DR. "A Heroine In Ebony." In *The Chautauquan. [Official Publication of Chautauqua Institution, a System of Popular Education].*, 459-62. Chautauqua, NY: Chautauqua Press, 1896.

Hyde, A. B. *The Story of Methodism throughout the World.* Springfield, MA: Wiley &, 1889. Google Books.

Ingalls, J. J. "*John Brown's Place in History.*" *The North American Review* 138 (February 1, 1884). Archive.org.

Ivers, Larry E. *British Drums on the Southern Frontier: The Military Colonization of Georgia, 1733-1749.* Chapel Hill: University of North Carolina Press, 1974.

Jacobs, Harriet A., Lydia Maria Child, and Jean Fagan. Yellin. *Incidents in the Life of a Slave Girl: Written by Herself.* Cambridge, MA: Harvard University Press, 1987.

"John Parker Hale (1806-1873)." Biographical Directory of the United States Congress, n.d.

Johnson, Andrew. "*What John Brown Did In Kansas.*" December 12, 1859. http://www.adena.com/adena/usa/cw/cw234.htm.

Jones, Charles C. *The History of Georgia.* Vol. 1-2. Boston: Houghton, Mifflin and, 1883. Archive.org.

Jones, George, ed. "Bringing Moravians to Georgia." Translated by David Noble. *The Georgia Historical Quarterly* 80, no. 4 (Winter 1996): 847-58. JSTOR.

Kaminski, John P. *A Necessary Evil? Slavery and the Debate over the Constitution.* Madison, WI: Madison House, 1995.

Kendrick, Stephen, and Paul Kendrick. *Sarah's Long Walk: the Free Blacks of Boston and How Their Struggle for Equality Changed America.* Boston: Beacon Press, 2004.

Kidd, Thomas S. *Patrick Henry: First among Patriots.* New York: Basic Books, 2011. Kindle Edition.

Klein, Herbert S. *The Atlantic Slave Trade.* Cambridge, U.K.: Cambridge University Press, 1999.

Langston, John Mercer. *From the Virginia Plantation to the National Capitol.* Hartford, CT: American Publishing Company, 1894.

Lawson, Edward. "What Became of the Man Who Cut Off Jenkin's Ear." *The Florida Historical Quarterly* 37, no. 1 (July 1958): 33-41. JSTOR.

Livermore, George. *Historical Research.* New York: J. Wilson and Son, 1862. *Google Books.*

Locke, Mary Stoughton. *Anti-Slavery in America: From the Introduction of African Slaves to the Prohibition of the Slave Trade, 1619-1808.* Gloucester, MA: Peter Smith, 1965.

Losada, Angel. "Bartolome de Las Casas Champion of Indian Rights in 16th Century." *The Courier,* June 1975.

Lovejoy, Joseph C., Owen Lovejoy, and John Quincy Adams. *Memoir of the Rev. Elijah P. Lovejoy; Who Was Murdered in Defense of the Liberty of the Press, at Alton, Illinois, Nov. 7, 1837.* New York: J.S. Taylor, 1838. Library of Congress. www.loc.gov.

Lovejoy, Owen, William F. Moore, and Jane Ann. Moore. *His Brother's Blood: Speeches and Writings, 1838-64 of Owen Lovejoy.* Urbana: University of Illinois Press, 2004.

Lowery, Woodbury. *The Spanish Settlements within the present limits of the United States 1513-1561;* Openlibrary.org. New York: The Knichvibocker Press, 1901.

Magdol, Edward. *Owen Lovejoy, Abolitionist in Congress.* New Brunswick, NJ: Rutgers University Press, 1967.

Marley, David. *Wars of the Americas: A Chronology of Armed Conflict in the Western Hemisphere, 1492 to the Present.* Santa Barbara, CA: ABC-CLIO, 2008.

Martin, Asa Earl. *The Anti-Slavery Movement in Kentucky Prior to 1850.* Google Books. Louisville: Standard Printing Company, 1918.

Mason, Thaddeus. *Biographical Memorials of James Oglethorpe.* Georgia: Georgia Historical Society, 1841. Kindle Edition.

Matlack, Rev Lucius C., and Rev D. D. Whedon. *The Antislavery Struggle and Triumph in the Methodist Episcopal Church.* Archive.org. New York: Phillips & Hunt, 1881.

Maxwell, John Francis. *Slavery and the Catholic Church. Forward by Lord Wilberforce.* Chichester: Rose. The Anti-Slavery Society for the Protection of Human Rights, 1975.

Meyer, Eugene. *Five for freedom: The African American soldiers in John Brown's Army.* Chicago: Lawrence Hill Books, 2018.

Meyer, Eugene. "Five Black Men Raided Harper's Ferry." *Washington Post,* October 13, 2019.

Moore, George Henry. *Notes on the History of Slavery in Massachusetts.* www.archive.org. New York: John F. Trow & Co, 1866.

Moore, Rev William F. "The Relationship Between Abraham Lincoln and Owen Lovejoy." www.Lovejoysociety.org. Speech presented at the Lincoln-Lovejoy Symposium, September 12, 1998.

Moore, William F., and Jane Ann. Moore. *Collaborators for Emancipation Abraham Lincoln and Owen Lovejoy.* Chicago: University of Illinois Press, 2014.

Morgan, David, Jr. "George Whitfield and the Great Awakening in the Carolinas and Georgia" 1739-1740." *Georgia Historical Quarterly* 54, no. 4 (Winter 1970): 517-39. JSTOR.

Nell, William C. *The Colored Patriots of the American Revolution.* Archive.org. Boston: R.F. Wallcut, 1855.

NY Times. "John P. Hale and His Work. The Statue of John P. Hale in Front of the Capitol and Presented to the State of New Hampshire by William E. Chandler. An Account of the Unveiling Ceremonies. Concord: Republican Press." The New York Times, November 12, 1893.

O'Connell, Neil. "George Whitefield and Bethesda Orphan House." *Georgia Historical Quarterly* 54, no. 1 (Spring 1970): 42-60. JSTOR.

Painter, Kyle. "The ProSlavery Argument in the Development of the American Methodist Church." *Constructing the Past,* 5th ser., 2, no. 1 (2001): 29-46.

Parker, Theodore. *The Trial of Theodore Parker: for the "Misdemeanor" of a Speech in Faneuil Hall Against Kidnapping, before the Circuit Court of the United States, at Boston, April 3, 1855.* Google Books. Boston: Self-Published, 1855.

Pettit, Eber M. *Sketches in the History of the Underground Railroad.* Www.archive.org. Fredonia, NY: w. McKinstry & Son, 1879.

Phillips, William D. *Slavery from Roman Times to the Early Transatlantic trade.* Minneapolis: University of Minnesota Press, 1985.

Proceedings of the Illinois Anti-Slavery Convention: Held at Upper Alton on October 26, 27, 28, 1837. Google Books. Alton: Parks and Breath, 1838.

Putnam, Mary. *The Baptists and Slavery.* Ann Arbor: George Wahr, 1913.

Quarles, Benjamin. *Black Abolitionists.* New York: Oxford University Press, 1969.

Quarles, Benjamin. *Blacks on John Brown.* Urbana, IL: University of Illinois Press, 1972.

Redpath, James. *The Public Life of Capt. John Brown,* Boston: Thayer and Eldridge, 1860. Archive.org.

Reynolds, David S. *John Brown, Abolitionist: The Man Who Killed Slavery, Sparked the Civil War, and Seeded Civil Rights.* New York: Alfred A. Knopf, 2005.

Richardson, Abby Sage. *The History of our Country from its Discovery by Columbus to the Celebration of the Centennial Anniversary of its Declaration of Independence.* Google Books. Boston: H.O. Houghton and Co., 1875.

Robinson, William. *"Warrington" Pen-Portraits: a Collection of Personal and Political Reminiscences from 1848 to 1876.* Ed. and Pub. by Mrs. W.S. Robinson, 1877.

Rodriguez, Junius P. *The Historical Encyclopedia of World Slavery.* Vol. 1–2. Santa Barbara, CA: ABC-CLIO, 1997.

Rodriguez, Junius P., and Orlando Patterson. *Chronology of World Slavery*. Santa Barbara, CA: ABC-CLIO, 1999.

Runyon, Randolph, and William Albert. Davis. *Delia Webster and the Underground Railroad*. Lexington: University Press of Kentucky, 1996.

Russell, John H. *The Free Negro in Virginia: 1619 - 1865*. Www.archive.org. Baltimore: Johns Hopkins Press, 1913.

Sanborn, Franklin Benjamin. *The Life and Letters of John Brown*. Boston: Roberts Bros, 1891. Google Books.

Sawyer, Kem Knapp. *The Underground Railroad in American History*. Springfield, NJ: Enslow Publishers, 1997.

Sewell, Richard H. *John P. Hale and the Politics of Abolition*. Cambridge: Harvard University Press, 1965.

Shurtleff, William. *A Letter to Those of His Brethren in the Ministry Who Refuse to Admit The Reverend Whitefield Into Their Pulpits*. Boston: Samuel Kneeland and Timothy Green, 1745. Google Books.

Siebert, Wilbur Henry. *The Underground Railroad from Slavery to Freedom*. New York: Macmillan, 1899. Google Books.

Smedley, R C. *History of the Underground Railroad in Chester and the Neighboring Counties of Pennsylvania*. Google Books. Lancaster, PA: John A. Hiestand, 1883.

Smith, Samuel Denny. *The Negro in Congress: 1870-1901*. Washington: Kennikat press, 1966.

Sloat, William A., II. "George Whitefield, African-Americans and Slavery." *Methodist History* 33, no. 1 (October 1994): 3-13.

Stein, Stephen. "George Whitefield on Slavery: Some New Evidence." *Church History* 42, no. 2 (June 1973): 243-56. JSTOR.

Stout, Harry. "Religion, Communications and the Idealogical Origins of the American Revolution." *William and Mary Quarterly* 34, no. 4 (October 1977): 519-41. JSTOR.

Still, William. *The Underground RailRoad*. Philadelphia: Porter & Coates, 1872. Kindle Edition.

Stowe, Harriet Beecher. *A key to Uncle Tom's Cabin; Presenting the Original Facts and Documents Upon Which the Story is Founded*. Boston: John P. Jewett & Co, 1853.

Strangis, Joel. *Lewis Hayden and the War Against Slavery*. Linnet Books, 1989.

Sumner, Charles. *The Crime against Kansas. Speech in Congress May 19, 1856,* Cleveland, Ohio: John P. Jewett &, 1856. Google Books.

Thompson, John. *The Life of John Thompson a Fugitive Slave: Containing His History of 25 Years in Bondage, and His Providential Escape*. Worcester: J. Thompson, 1856. Google Books.

Thomas, Hugh. *The Slave Trade: the Story of the Atlantic Slave Trade, 1440-1870*. New York: Simon & Schuster, 1997.

Thomas, Hugh. *Rivers of Gold: The Rise of the Spanish Empire, from Columbus to Magellan*. New York: Random House, 2003.

Thompson, John. *The Life of John Thompson a Fugitive Slave: Containing His History of 25 Years in Bondage, and His Providential Escape*. Google Books. Worcester: J. Thompson, 1856.

Tipple, Ezra S. *Francis Asbury: The Prophet of the Long Road*. Cincinnati: Methodist Book Concern, 1916. Google Books.

Tobboy, Stanley, and Anita Robboy. "Lewis Hayden: From Fugitive Slave to Statesman." *New England Quarterly* 46, no. 4 (December 1973): 591–613.

Tomkins, Stephen. *John Wesley: A Biography*. Grand Rapids, MI: Wm. B. Eerdmans Pub., 2003.

Tyerman, Luke. *The Life and Times of the Rev. John Wesley, M.A., Founder of the Methodists.* Vol. 1-2. New York: Harper & Bros., 1872. Google Books.

Tyerman, Luke. *The Life of the Rev. George Whitefield.* Vol. 1-2. New York: Randolph, 1877. Google Books.

Urbainczyk, Theresa. *Slave Revolts in Antiquity.* Berkeley: University of California Press, 2008.

U. S. Congress. *Congressional Globe,* 31st Congress Session 1, 1850. p. 515.

Wesley, John. *The Works of the Rev. John Wesley, A.M.* Edited by John Emory. Vol. 1-7. New York: Mason & Lane, 1840. Google Books.

Whitefield, George. *A Letter to the Reverend John Wesley To Answer His Sermon on Free Grace.* London: Strahan, 1741. Google Books.

"Who Was the Hon. Rev Owen Glendower Lovejoy?" Lovejoy Society, n.d.

Wiencek, Henry. *An Imperfect God: George Washington, His Slaves, and the Creation of America.* New York: Farrar, Straus and Giroux, 2003.

Wilberforce, Robert Isaac, and Samuel Wilberforce. *The Life of William Wilberforce.* Vol. 1-5. London: J. Murray, 1838. Google Books.

Williams, Robert. *George Whitefield's Bethesda: The Orphanage, The College and the Library.* 1968. Library History Seminar No. 3, Proceedings, Georgia.

U.S. Congress. Bill, Globe §. 597 (1851).

Villard, Oswald Garrison. *John Brown, 1800-1859. A Biography Fifty Years After.* Houghton Mifflin Company: Boston, 1910. Google Books.

Williams, George W. A History of the Negro Troops in the War of the Rebellion, 1861-1865, 1888.

Willis H. Hughes v William Craft: (U.S. Circuit Court for the District of Massachusetts October 25, 1850).

www.research.archives.gov. Online Public Access to National Archives.

Wilson, Henry. *History of the Antislavery Measures of the Thirty-Seventh and Thirty-Eighth United States Congresses, 1861-64.* Boston: Walker, 1864.

Wilson, Henry. *History of the Reconstruction Measures of the Thirty-ninth and Fortieth Congresses, 1865-68.* Archive.org. Hartford: Hartford Pub. Co., 1868.

Wilson, Henry. *History of the Rise and Fall of the Slave Power in America.* Vol. 1–3. Boston: J.R. Osgood and Co., 1872.

References

1. ^ Craft, William and Ellen. *Running a Thousand Miles,* page iii. All quotations in this chapter come from the autobiography of William and Ellen Craft.
2. ^ Ibid, 1.
3. ^ Ibid, 27-28.
4. ^ Ibid, 2.
5. ^ Ibid, 32-33.
6. ^ Ibid, 34-35.
7. ^ Ibid, 30.
8. ^ Ibid, 40.
9. ^ Ibid, 42.
10. ^ Ibid, 43.
11. ^ Ibid, 2-10.
12. ^ Ibid, 40.
13. ^ Ibid, 40.
14. ^ Ibid, 46.
15. ^ Ibid, 47.
16. ^ Ibid 47-49.
17. ^ Ibid 57-58.
18. ^ Ibid, 61-62.
19. ^ Ibid, 69.
20. ^ Ibid, 69-72.
21. ^ Ibid, 80.
22. ^ Ibid, 2.
23. ^ Ibid, 82.
24. ^ Ibid, 16-28.
25. ^ Tobboy, Stanley, and Anita Robboy. "Lewis Hayden," 593.
26. ^ Strangis, Joel. The War, 5 & Tobboy, Stanley, and Anita Robboy. "Lewis Hayden," 592.
27. ^ Stowe, Harriet Beecher, Key, 155.
28. ^ Runyon, Randolph, and William Albert. Davis. Delia Webster, 113-115.

29.   ^ Ibid.

30.   ^ Runyon, Randolph, and William Albert. Davis. *Delia Webster,* 9 & Strangis, Joel. *The War,* 16.

31.   ^ Runyon, Randolph, and William Albert. Davis. *Delia Webster,* 37 & Strangis, Joel. *The War, 33-34.*

32.   ^ Runyon, Randolph, and William Albert. Davis. *Delia Webster,* 92 & Strangis, Joel. *The War,* 43.

33.   ^ Strangis, Joel. *The War,* 43.

34.   ^ Chapman, Maria, *Right and Wrong,* 102-110 & Garrison, Wendell. *William Lloyd Garrison,* Vol 2. 273.

35.   ^ Lincoln, *Lost Speech,* 46-47.

36.   ^ Strangis, Joel. *The War,* 61.

37.   ^ Ibid.

38.   ^ Collison, Gary Lee. Shadrach Minkins, 96.

39.   ^ Declaration of Colored People of Boston

40.   ^ Declaration of the *Colored* Citizens of Boston & Strangis, Joel. The War, 64-66.

41.   ^ Collison, Gary Lee. Shadrach Minkins, 79 & Strangis, Joel. *The War* 61. Note: this is NOT the Joseph Smith who founded Mormonism and died in 1844.

42.   ^ Declaration of the *Colored* Citizens of Boston & Strangis, Joel. The War, 64-66.

43.   ^ Collison, Gary Lee. *Shadrach Minkins,* 95.

44.   ^ Runyon, Randolph, and William Albert. Davis. *Delia Webster,* 142 & Tobboy, Stanley, and Anita Robboy. "Lewis Hayden" 600-601.

45.   ^ Quarles, Benjamin, *Black Abolitionists,* 203.

46.   ^ Collison, Gary Lee. *Shadrach Minkins,* 99.

47.   ^ Collison, Gary Lee. *Shadrach Minkins,* 121.

48.   ^ Collison, Gary Lee. *Shadrach Minkins,* 123.

49.   ^ Ibid, 135.

50.   ^ Globe, 31st Congress, Session 2, p. 596-599.

51.   ^ Ibid.

52.   ^ Ibid.

53.   ^ Collision, Gary. "This Flagitious Offense." 610.

54.   ^ Collision, Gary. "This Flagitious Offense." 610 & *Shadrach Minkins,* 140 & Strangis, Joel. *The War,* 77.

55.   ^ Wilson, *Rise,* Vol 2. p. 333 & Robinson, William. *Pen-Portraits,* 71-72 and William Chandler, *Statue of John P. Hale,* 171-172.

56.   ^ Robinson, William. *Pen-Portraits,* 71-72.

57.   ^ Chandler, William, *Statute of John P. Hale*, 171-172.

58.   ^ Kendrick, Stephen, and Paul Kendrick. *Sarah's Long Walk*, 221.

59.   ^ Aptheker, Herbert, *Documentary History*, 370-371.

60.   ^ Strangis, Joel. *The War*, 138.

61.   ^ Ibid, 137.

62.   ^ Ibid, 141.

63.   ^ Gledstone, James. *The Life and Travels of George Whitefield*, 50 & Goodell, William. *Slavery*, 20-21.

64.   ^ When Charles Dickens was growing up in the early 1800's, his parents ended up in debtor's prison, forcing him to drop out of school and get a job at age twelve. The humiliation he experienced later inspired him to write the classic novel *A Christmas Carol*.

65.   ^ Jones, *Bringing Moravians*, 857.

66.   ^ Cate, Margaret. "Fort Frederica." 133, 171.

67.   ^ Cate, Margaret. "Fort Frederica." 133, 171.

68.   ^ Ibid, 134.

69.   ^ Ibid, 157.

70.   ^ Ibid, 161.

71.   ^ Ibid, 165.

72.   ^ Ibid, 171-172.

73.   ^ Jones, Charles. *History of Georgia*, Vol 1. p. 203-207.

74.   ^ Ibid, 287.

75.   ^ Ibid, 288.

76.   ^ Tomkins, Stephen. *John Wesley*, 58.

77.   ^ Wesley, John. *Works*, (1840 edition edited by John Emory) Vol 2. p. 335-336.

78.   ^ Jones, Charles. *History of Georgia*, Vol 1. p. 402.

79.   ^ Henry, Stuart Clark. *George Whitefield: Wayfaring Witness*, 51.

80.   ^ Franklin, Benjamin. *Autobiography*, 90-91.

81.   ^ Cousins, *In God We Trust*, 252-253.

82.   ^ Tyerman, Luke. *The Life of the Rev. George Whitefield*, Vol 1. p. 339-440 & George Whitefield, *Letter to John Wesley*, 1-31.

83.   ^ Henry, Stuart Clark. *George Whitefield: Wayfaring Witness*, 96.

84.   ^ Aldridge, Alfred. "George Whitefield's Georgia Controversies." 369.

85.   ^ Franklin, Benjamin. *Autobiography*, 90-91.

86.   ^ Ibid.

87.   ^ Henry, Stuart Clark. *George Whitefield: Wayfaring Witness*, 56.

88.   ^ Aldridge, Alfred. "George Whitefield's Georgia Controversies." 370.

89.   ^ Gledstone, James Paterson. The Life and Travels of George Whitefield, 391-392, 433-434 & Stephen Stein "George Whitefield on Slavery." 245.

90.   ^ Gledstone, James Paterson. The Life and Travels of George Whitefield, 391-392, 433-434 & Stephen Stein "George Whitefield on Slavery." 245.

91.   ^ Jones, Charles. History of Georgia, Vol 1. p. 419.

92.   ^ Goodell, William. Slavery, 21.

93.   ^ Livermore, Historical Research, 18.

94.   ^ Livermore, Historical Research, 18.

95.   ^ Declaration of Independence.

96.   ^ Kaminski, Necessary Evil? 163.

97.   ^ Matlack and Whedon. The Antislavery Struggle and Triumph in the Methodist Episcopal Church, 58-60.

98.   ^ Thompson, John. Life, 18-86.

99.   ^ Aptheker, Herbert. American Negro Slave Revolts, 102-107.

100.   ^ Matlack and Whedon. The Antislavery Struggle and Triumph in the Methodist Episcopal Church, 66-67.

101.   ^ Asbury, Francis. Journal, Vol 1. 280 & Hirschfeld, George Washington and Slavery, 203.

102.   ^ John Kaminski, Necessary Evil? 33-34.

103.   ^ Hardin, William. Litigating the Lash, 152 & Kaminski, Necessary Evil? 36.

104.   ^ Wilberforce, Robert Isaac, and Samuel Wilberforce. Life, Vol 1. p. 297.

105.   ^ Lovejoy et al. His Brother's Blood, 2-3.

106.   ^ Magdol, Edward, Owen Lovejoy, 8.

107.   ^ Lovejoy, et. al, Memoir, 185-186.

108.   ^ Magdol, Edward, Owen Lovejoy, 19-20.

109.   ^ Magdol, Edward, Owen Lovejoy, 15.

110.   ^ Ibid, 21.

111.   ^ Lovejoy et al., Memoir, 2-12.

112.   ^ Magdol, Edward. Owen Lovejoy, 33.

113.   ^ Isaiah 16:3 (NET)

114.   ^ Lovejoy, et al. His Brother's Blood, 20-23.

Lovejoy is quoting several Bible verses including the story of Daniel in the lion's den (Daniel 6:22) and Shadrach and his friends getting thrown in the fiery furnace (Daniel 3:16-28). Then Lovejoy is also quoting Jesus' warning about hell in Matthew 10:28 and Mark 9:48.

115.   ^ Magdol, Lovejoy, 41.

116.   ^ Magdol, Lovejoy, 44.

117.   ^ Lovejoy et al. His Brother's Blood, 25-32.

118. ^ Magdol, Edward. *Lovejoy,* 73.

119. ^ Magdol, Edward. *Lovejoy,* 76.

120. ^ Magdol, Edward. *Lovejoy,* 93.

121. ^ Brewster, Rebekah, *Christians That Fought Slavery,* 259.

122. ^ Lovejoy et al. *His Brother's Blood,* 146-147.

123. ^ Moore, William and Jane Ann, *Collaborators for Emancipation,* 74.

124. ^ Lovejoy et al. *His Brother's Blood,* 166-178. Lovejoy is quoting 1Samuel 17:5 where David threatens to kill Goliath.

125. ^ Lovejoy et al. *His Brother's Blood,* 191-208.

126. ^ Lovejoy et al. *His Brother's Blood,* 192-211.

127. ^ Lovejoy et al. *His Brother's Blood,* 193 & Magdol, *Owen Lovejoy,* 234.

128. ^ Lovejoy et al. *His Brother's Blood,* 192-211. Lovejoy might have been joking when he referenced 1Timothy 4:11. The official record says that Congressmen burst out laughing when he said this.

129. ^ Moore, William and Janet. *Collaborators for Emancipation,* 93 and Magdol, *Owen Lovejoy,* 237.

130. ^ Lovejoy et al. *His Brother's Blood,* 160.

131. ^ Lovejoy et al. *His Brother's Blood,* 161.

132. ^ Moore, *Collaborators,* 97.

133. ^ Lovejoy et al, *His Brother's Blood,* 250-261

134. ^ Wilson, *Anti-Slavery Measures,* 93.

135. ^ Moore. *Collaborators,* 140.

136. ^ Ibid.

137. ^ Lovejoy, et al. *His Brother's Blood,* 354.

138. ^ Lovejoy, et al. *His Brother's Blood,* 329-349.

139. ^ Lovejoy, et al. *His Brother's Blood,* 410.

140. ^ Lovejoy, et al. *His Brother's Blood,* 411.

141. ^ Sewell, *John P. Hale,* 58.

142. ^ Ibid, 33.

143. ^ Ibid, 114-115.

144. ^ Ibid, 131.

145. ^ Ibid, 63.

146. ^ Ibid, 71.

147. ^ Ibid, 71.

148. ^ Ibid, 73-74.

149. ^ Ibid, 123.

150. ^ Ibid, 140.

151. ^ Ibid, 142.

152. ^ Chandler, William, Statute of John P. Hale, 171-172.

153.   ^ Ibid, 161.
154.   ^ Ibid, 165-166.
155.   ^ Ibid, 39.
156.   ^ Ibid, 137-138
157.   ^ Ibid, 138.
158.   ^ Congressional Globe, 31st Congress, p. 515.
159.   ^ Ibid, 138.
160.   ^ Ibid, 212.
161.   ^ Ibid, 212-213.
162.   ^ Ibid, 234.
163.   ^ Sanborn, Franklin, *Life and Letters,* 52-53.
164.   ^ Villard, Oswald. *Fifty Years After,* 47.
165.   ^ Sanborn, *Life and Letters,* 620-621.
166.   ^ Ibid, 598.
167.   ^ Ibid, 526.
168.   ^ Villard, Fifty Years After, 74.
169.   ^ Wilson, *Rise,* Vol 2, p. 466.
170.   ^ Wilson, *Rise,* Vol 2, p. 468 & James Redpath, *Public Life,* 77-78.
171.   ^ Wilson, *Rise,* Vol 2, p. 468
172.   ^ Ibid, 467.
173.   ^ Sanborn, *Letters,* 190.
174.   ^ Ibid, 206.
175.   ^ Sumner, Charles. The Crime against Kansas, 27-28.
176.   ^ Sanborn, *Letters,* 188.
177.   ^ Ibid.
178.   ^ Villard, Fifty Years After, 83-84.
179.   ^ Sanborn, *Letters,* 190.
180.   ^ Villard, Fifty Years After, 90.
181.   ^ Ibid, 84, 110-111.
182.   ^ Sanborn, *Letters,* 256.
183.   ^ Villard, Fifty Years After, 93 & J.J. Ingalls, "Brown's Place in History."
184.   ^ Sanborn, *Letters,* 260.
185.   ^ Villard, Fifty Years After, 137.
186.   ^ Sanborn, *Letters,* 259.
187.   ^ Redpath, James. *Public Life,* 183.
188.   ^ Redpath, James. *Public Life,* 117.
189.   ^ Sanborn, *Letters,* 260.
190.   ^ Sanborn, *Letters,* 272.
191.   ^ Villard, Fifty Years After, 156.
192.   ^ Sanborn, *Letters,* 255-256.

193.   ^ Sanborn, *Letters,* 234.

194.   ^ Villard, Fifty Years After, 182.

195.   ^ Villard, Fifty Years After, 154.

196.   ^ Redpath, James, 118.

197.   ^ Ibid.

198.   ^ Sanborn, *Letters,* 257.

199.   ^ Villard, *Fifty Years After,* 151-153.

200.   ^ Sanborn, *Letters,* 266-267, 272.

201.   ^ Villard, Fifty Years After, 154.

202.   ^ Ingalls, J. J. "John Brown's Place in History." 146.

203.   ^ Villard, *Fifty Years After,* 182-183.

204.   ^ Redpath, James. *Public Life,* 227.

205.   ^ Sanborn, *Letters,* 272.

206.   ^ Ibid, 237-240.

207.   ^ Ibid, 244.

208.   ^ Villard, Fifty Years After, 214.

209.   ^ Ibid.

210.   ^ Ibid.

211.   ^ Redpath, *Public Life,* 157.

212.   ^ Sanborn, *Letters,* 278.

213.   ^ Villard, Fifty Years After, 263.

214.   ^ Redpath, *Public Life,* 160-168.

215.   ^ Ibid, 176-184.

216.   ^ Clinton, Catherine. *Road to Freedom,* 141

217.   ^ Sanborn, *Letters,* 420-421 & Villard, *Fifty Years After,* 48.

218.   ^ Redpath, *Public Life,* 206.

219.   ^ Sanborn, *Letters,* 419-420.

220.   ^ Ibid, 538-540.

221.   ^ Sanborn, *Letters,* 512.

222.   ^ Redpath, *Public Life,* 48.

223.   ^ Bradford, Sarah, *Harriett,* 134.

224.   ^ Bradford, Sarah, *Harriett,* 118.

225.   ^ Sanborn, *Letters,* 503-504.

226.   ^ Ibid, 485-487.

227.   ^ Sanborn, *Letters,* 485.

228.   ^ Anderson, *Voice,* 24.

229.   ^ Ibid, 5.

230.   ^ Sanborn, *Letters,* 540-541.

231.   ^ Langston, John, *From Plantation To National Capital,* 193.

232.   ^ Anderson, *Voice,* 29.

233.   ^ Ibid, 31.

234.   ^ Ibid, 35.

235.   ^ Sanborn, *Letters,* 549.

236.   ^ Anderson, *Voice,* 42.

237.   ^ Ibid, 40.

238.   ^ Ibid, 49.

239.   ^ Ibid, 50, 60

240.   ^ Redpath, *Public Life,* 269.

241.   ^ Villard, *Fifty Years After,* 498-499.

242.   ^ Redpath, *Public Life,* 357.

243.   ^ Sanborn, *Letters,* 358.

244.   ^ Redpath, *Public Life,* 359.

245.   ^ Redpath, *Public Life,* 354.

246.   ^ Redpath, *Public Life,* 359.

247.   ^ Anderson, *Voice,* 6.

248.   ^ Quarles, Benjamin. *Blacks on John Brown,* 102-103.

Bible Versions

About The Author

Rebekah Brewster is a professional writer who loves making words come alive on the page. She is a California girl with a Midwestern heart. Her hobbies include reading lots of books, cooking and hiking on nature trails.

Rebekah loves this country and all those that sacrifice for it. She also cares deeply about her readers. She hopes this book inspires you to be strong during troubled times. Never give up while you are suffering because each day you are closer to the answer.

If you enjoyed the book, please leave a good review on the website where purchased. If you want Rebekah to speak at your church, email her at Info@Quietbeauty.org.